ROBIN SHARMA
THE GREATNESS GUIDE, BOOK 2

101 Lessons for Success and Happiness

HarperCollins*Publishers*Ltd

The Greatness Guide, Book 2
© 2007 by Robin Sharma. All rights reserved.

Published by HarperCollins Publishers Ltd

Originally published by HarperCollins Publishers Ltd
in a hardcover edition: 2007
This trade paperback edition: 2008

HarperCollins books may be purchased for educational, business, or sales promotional use through our Special Markets Department.

HarperCollins Publishers Ltd
2 Bloor Street East, 20th Floor
Toronto, Ontario, Canada
M4W 1A8

www.harpercollins.ca

Library and Archives Canada Cataloguing in Publication
information is available.

ISBN 978-1-55468-403-8

The Greatness Guide, Book 2 is printed on Ancient Forest Friendly paper,
made with 100% post-consumer waste.

Printed and bound in the Canada
STJ 9 8 7 6 5 4 3 2 1

Set in Dante and Univers

*To the Dreamers amongst us—those brave souls
willing to ignore the chattering voices of their critics in passionate
pursuit of their highest ideals. You are the Great Ones.*

CONTENTS

*"Our lives begin to end the day
we become silent about things that matter."*
MARTIN LUTHER KING, JR.

1

BE THE BEST YOU

Warren Buffet once observed, "There will never be a better you than you." Brilliant insight. From a brilliant guy. There will never be a better me than me. And there will never be a better you than you. Some might try to copy the way you think, speak and act. But no matter how hard they try, they will only be a second-best you. Because you are unique. Only one of you alive today. Among the billions of us. Makes you stop and think, doesn't it? Makes you realize you are pretty special. No, very special. And that there really isn't any competition.

And so today, what will you do with you as you march out into a world that needs people playing at extraordinary with their lives more than ever before? Will you exert more of your hidden potential? Will you liberate more of your natural creativity? Will you uncover more of your authenticity? And will you be more of the you that you are meant to be? Just wondering. Because there will never be a better time to be the best you than today. And if not now, then when? Makes me think of what the philosopher Herodotus once said: "It is better by noble boldness to run the risk of being subject to half of the evils we anticipate than to remain in cowardly listlessness for fear of what may happen." So beautifully said.

---

*There will never be a better time
to be the best you than today.*

2

INVISIBLE FENCES

I'm sitting here at the airport in Los Angeles. Was here to speak to a group of General Electric's high-potential employees. About Leading Without Title. About standing for world-class. About outright Greatness in all they do.

After the presentation I reflected on why so many of us play small in the core areas of our lives. Why we avoid change. Why we don't innovate and express the creative genius that resides within each one of us. Why we refuse to accept the call on our lives. And why so many of us refrain from being remarkable. The answer I came up with? Invisible Fences.

Here's what I'm talking about: I took a drive out into the countryside last week. To breathe. To renew. To think. I saw a sign from a dog training company on someone's lawn. It spoke of an Invisible Fence. It's a system that sets an invisible boundary that the dog can't get past. The dog eventually becomes conditioned so that even when that fence is gone, it will not run beyond it. The dog sets up imaginary limits that determine its reality. We're like that too. As we grow up, we adopt negative beliefs and false assumptions and sabotaging fears from the world around us. These become our Invisible

Fences. We believe they are real. When we bump up against them at work (and in life), we retreat. We believe the boundary is true. So we shrink from all we are meant to be/do/have. The illusion seems so real. But it's not. Please remember that.

So I invite you to question your Invisible Fences. Be aware of them. Observe them. Challenge them. So that when one confronts you, rather than running away from it, you exercise the force of will and talent of heart to run through it. Toward the poetic possibilities your life is meant to be. Because what you resist will persist. But what you befriend, you will transcend.

As we grow up, we adopt negative beliefs and false assumptions and sabotaging fears from the world around us. These become our Invisible Fences.

3

THE POWER OF SIMPLE

I learn so much from my children. Not only are they my heroes—
they are two of my best teachers. They have shown me how to live
in the moment, helped me to see life as an adventure and taught
me how to open my heart. And they've taught me so many lessons
on The Power of Simple. These days, I'm all about simple. A simple message about everyone being a leader—no matter what they
do or who they are. Simple ideas and tools (that actually work) to
help people and organizations get to world class. And living a far
simpler life (because, at heart, I'm a very simple man). Simple, to
me, is so powerful (Google co-founder Sergey Brin made the point
superbly when he said that at his company "Success will come
from simplicity.") Which brings me to Colby, my son.

We went to New York City a few weeks ago. A shared experience that we'd planned for a long time; it was all about celebrating
his thirteenth birthday (a kid only becomes a teenager once). We
hung out in SoHo. Went toy shopping at FAO Schwarz. Had a beautiful lunch at Bread (one of my favorite lunch places on earth). And
saw the great play *Wicked*. A weekend full of precious pleasures and
unforgettable memories. Between a father and his son.

Sunday night, on the flight home, I asked my young buddy, "What did you like best about our weekend?" He sat silently. Thought deeply. Then he smiled. "Dad, you know that hot dog you bought me on the street yesterday? I loved that the most." The Power of Simple.

Success will come from simplicity.

4

BE SO GOOD THEY CAN'T IGNORE YOU

Here's comedian Steve Martin's advice to young comics: "Be so good they can't ignore you." Love it. Life favors the devoted. The more you give to life, the more life sends back. It's just not possible for you to be great at what you do, always reaching for your brilliance and standing for excellence, and not win in the end. (Jerry Garcia of The Grateful Dead once said, "You do not merely want to be the best of the best. You want to be considered the only ones who do what you do.")

Sometimes discouragement sets in. Happens to all of us. We try hard, stay true to our dreams and pursue our ideals. Yet nothing happens. Or so it seems. But every choice matters. And every step counts. Life runs according to its own agenda, not ours. Be patient. Trust. Be like the stonecutter, steadily chipping away, day after day. Eventually, a single blow will crack the stone and reveal the diamond. An enthusiastic, dedicated person who is ridiculously good at what they do just cannot be denied. Seriously.

Steve Martin's insight speaks to me deeply. "Be so good they can't ignore you." (Management guru Peter Drucker made the point slightly differently when he observed: "Get good or get out.") Apply that philosophy at work. Apply it at home. Apply it in your community. Apply it to your world. Having the courage to present your gifts and your highest capacities will yield magnificent rewards. Life is always fair in the end. Trust it.

Life is always fair in the end. Trust it.

5

THE SUCCESS EXPANSION PRINCIPLE

Here's a powerful idea that just might revolutionize the way you work and live if you embrace it at a DNA level: Your life will expand or contract in direct relationship to your willingness to walk directly toward the things that you fear. Do your fears and you'll shine. Run away from them and you shrink from greatness. Reminds me of what Frank Herbert wrote in *Dune*: "I must not fear. Fear is the mind-killer. Fear is the little death that brings total obliteration. I will face my fear. I will permit it to pass over me and through me. And when it has gone past I will turn the inner eye to see its path. Where the fear has gone there will be nothing. Only I will remain."

So amazing what happens when you encounter a situation that makes you feel uncomfortable/insecure/scared and yet, instead of heading for the metaphorical exit door, you stay strong and do the thing you know you should do. First, you realize that the fear was mostly a hallucination. And second, you get some kind of unexpected reward for your bravery, because on the other side of every fear door lie gorgeous gifts, including personal growth, confidence and wisdom. I've seen it time and time again.

It's a law of life, I guess. So run toward fear. Start small. Slow and steady always wins the race. And watch the success you so dearly deserve begin to show up. When you most need it.

On the other side of every fear door
lie gorgeous gifts.

6

WEAR SHINY SHOES

Okay, your shoes don't need to shine for you to be a superb leader. And please remember, leadership isn't about your position, it's a way of being—Leading Without Title, to be precise. Leadership is about holding yourself to world-class standards, taking personal responsibility (versus playing the victim), being excellent within the sphere of your influence, building beautiful relationships and elevating others by your example. My point with this chapter is simply this: The way you do the little things says a lot about the way you will do the big things. And resigning yourself to mediocrity around your minor pursuits sets you up for mediocrity when it comes to the major ones.

If your yard or home is well organized, I'll bet your life is well organized. If you are attentive to details like remembering the birthdays of your friends and sending thank-you notes after every meeting, my guess is that you will be attentive to the details around your larger projects and bigger opportunities. And if your place of business is spotless, there's a great chance the work you do for your customers will reflect the same commitment to excellence. (I can tell a lot about a business by the cleanliness of their bathrooms; an immaculate bathroom shouts "We care!" and that caring translates into remarkable service.)

So pay attention to the details. Focus on the small stuff (like crazy). Commit to OAD: Obsessive Attention to Detail. World-class people and organizations always do. Because the little things truly are the big ones.

My point is simply this:
The way you do the little things
says a lot about the way you will
do the big things.

7

LISTEN CAREFULLY

Just read these immensely important words of celebrated designer Bruce Mau that I need to share with you: "Every collaborator who enters our orbit brings with him or her a world more strange and complex than any we could ever hope to imagine. By listening to the details and the subtlety of their needs, desires, or ambitions, we fold their world onto our own. Neither party will ever be the same."

We are shaped by our conversations. We are influenced by the ideas we hear and the people we meet. (Big idea: Every person you meet knows at least one thing you don't; don't let them leave without learning it.) Listening is a master skill for personal and professional excellence. Leaders listen. Staggeringly well. Mau's absolutely right: When we go deep into listening to the person we are communicating with, when we allow them to share what they know, we have the opportunity to get behind their eyeballs and learn, grow and evolve into our highest and best. And if you are lucky enough to be talking to the right person—at the right time—that single conversation might be the one that changes the way you think, feel and behave forever. Their stardust will rub off on you. And you'll be transformed. For good.

Every person you meet knows at least one thing you don't; don't let them leave without learning it.

8

DREAM LIKE DAVID

There's a man I wish you could meet. I was introduced to him while I was in Mexico City to deliver a speech to business and social leaders. He moved me with his story. And he humbled me by his courage.

David Mejia was born without ears. Doctors predicted he would suffer from poor hearing throughout his childhood and that he would be unlikely to live a full adult life. His youth was riddled with operation after operation, a great deal of pain, and the hurtful taunts of classmates who made fun of his appearance. But David persevered. Greatness, in so many ways, is determined by whether you persist through failure or let it consume you. David dreamed. He worked hard. And he believed. Because he knew he was meant to do extraordinary things.

David Mejia has been blessed. With a powerful mind. With a big heart. With a strong spirit. And with wonderful parents, who told him on a near-daily basis that if he looked for the best from life, he would find it. They encouraged him never to play victim. Told him to find the opportunity amid his challenges. And so he has. Masterfully.

The man I met in Mexico City is a leader. A hero. An inspiration. Why? Because he has taken what life sent him and turned what most of us would spend our days crying about into gold. He now has prosthetic ears. He's healthy and remarkably vital. He has achieved superb success in his career. He has found great love and joy. He has more friends than most people I know (far more than me). And he is stunningly positive in a world where people who have nothing to complain about spend most of their time complaining about trivialities.

You can curse the darkness, or you can light a candle and show up as a leader. Life is all about how you exercise the choices available to you. And your daily choices stack up to craft your destiny. Day by day. Week by week. Month by month. Year by year. David Mejia knows how to make the choices that will raise him to his own personal mountaintop. So do you.

You can curse the darkness, or you can light a candle and show up as a leader.

17

9

DO IT NOW

Woke up this morning with the following line from Mick Jagger's solo album *Goddess in the Doorway* screaming through my head: "No use getting misty eyed, it all screams by so fast." True. Life really does scream by.

Why postpone what you can do today to some time off in the distance? Why put off playing your greatest game as a human being to some point in the future? Why delay having a remarkably good time until you are old? The other day I read about a young woman who was reflecting on her retirement savings plan. She said, "I want to make sure I've saved up a lot—that way I can have at least some fun at the end of my life." I don't get it. Why wait until you are old to love living?

I'm in no way suggesting that you neglect the importance of planning for your future. Take the long view and prepare for a full life. As always, it's a balance. Do your plans. Save for retirement. Be strategic. But at the same time, live in the moment. Play full out. Take daily risks. Smart. Emirates Airlines has an ad that asks: "When was the last time you did something for the first time?" Smart.

So fill your days with color. Hunt for the best that this very day will bring. Laugh a lot. Love a lot. Dream a lot. And if there's an opportunity that the coming hours present to you—and we both know there will be—seize it. Because life screams by. So fast.

Why delay having a remarkably good time until you are old?

10

JBN (JUST BE NICE)

Question for you: Why don't we see being "noticeably nice" written into any job descriptions? There's a ton of stuff in those descriptions about what needs to get done each day, but nice is just an accessory, it seems. An add-on. An afterthought. I don't get it.

I believe that being nice is, in many ways, the very lifeblood of a world-class business. Being nice to teammates (so they love coming to work each day) attracts and retains superb talent. Being nice to your suppliers (so they go to the wall for you) is excellent for operations. And being nice to your customers (so they keep coming back) is the best way to grow your community of loyal and passionate followers. Nice is what builds enduring businesses. Here's an example.

Went to my local deli yesterday. Felt like some protein and veggies for lunch. I was in an ultra-creative mode and wanted to feed my brain well. I decided on a portion of turkey and a snow pea salad. I asked for what I wanted. The young woman behind the counter replied with a smile, "The rule is to sell the turkeys whole but I'm going to go see if I can break it for you." A minute later, I had my piece of turkey. She added with a wink, "I'll give you the one with the most seasoning—you'll love it." And on it went. Helping me. Wowing me. Being stunningly kind to me. A delicious experience of exceptional customer service. Because she was uncommonly nice.

Guess where I had lunch today? I returned there because, like most human beings, I do business with people who treat me well. Who doesn't want to help the nice ones succeed? Nice got my loyalty. It got my repeat business. It generated an evangelist. To world-class businesses, nice matters. So JBN. Daily.

Nice is what builds enduring businesses.

11

THERE ARE NO MISTAKES

It's so easy to beat yourself up over mistakes you've made. Too many among us live in the past rather than loving the present and building a dazzlingly bright future. Some people stay stuck for years over something they did or a failure they experienced. Sad. A life is a terrible thing to waste.

But let me ask you a question: Is there really such a thing as a mistake? First of all, no one tries to fail or mess things up. Every one of us wakes up in the morning, walks out into the world and does the best we can do based on what we know, the skills we have and where we are on life's journey. But even more importantly, every so-called mistake is actually a rich source of learning. An opportunity to build more awareness and understanding and gain precious experience. Experience that will help us do, feel and be even better. Everything that has happened to you in your life—the good and the difficult—was necessary to help you become the person you are now. Why make it wrong? So, just maybe, there are no mistakes. Just maybe what we could call failures are actually growth lessons in wolf's clothing. And just maybe the person who experiences the most wins.

Everything that has happened to you in your life—the good and the difficult—was necessary to help you become the person you are now.

12

THE BLANK SLATE OF TOMORROW

At midnight tonight, you'll get a most amazing gift: a fresh set of 24 hours. These hours are pure and flawless and limitless. They offer you the opportunity to show courage, behave brilliantly, connect compassionately, and forge those new habits of mastery that will get you to a better place of being. And they offer you a space to laugh. To create value. And to do your dreams. Whether you'll admit it or not, tomorrow is incredible. Not everyone gets one.

I just got home from Kazakhstan. Loved my time there. Almaty is such a beautiful city, surrounded by those mountains, and those apple trees. Filled with truly delightful people and rich with unforgettable culture. The leadership seminar I delivered was such a joy for me. On the long flight back, I read Peter Mayle's book *A Good Year*. I had enjoyed *A Year in Provence*, so I thought I'd find this one relaxing—and I did. It's a perfect vacation-reading book. One line in the work struck me: "It's better to die standing than live your whole life on your knees." Unbelievably powerful phrase. Thanks, Peter Mayle. For waking me up. To what's most important.

So make tomorrow special. No, make it outrageously great. Wildly wonderful. A piece of art—one that you can tell your grandkids about. Just amazing what one can do in a single day. Each one is a chance to be more of what we are all designed to be.

"It's better to die standing than live your whole life on your knees."

13

GET GREAT AT GRATITUDE

A while ago on CNN's *Larry King Live*, King interviewed Carolyn Thomas, who lost most of her face when her ex-boyfriend shot it off. There she sat, with bandages, one eye and more courage than I've seen in a long time.

This got me thinking about gratitude. Powerful idea: What you value in your life increases in value. What you think about and focus on grows. What you appreciate begins to appreciate. Appreciate your good health. Appreciate your family. Appreciate your gifts, your friends, your work and your life, and your perception will begin to shift. You'll see the blessings of your life (versus the broken parts).

I'm big on lists. My suggestion for you: List 50 things you are grateful for (yes, 50). The first 10 are easy: loved ones, job, home, etc. But go down to the roots. Dig (the pearls always require deep diving). Be grateful for the fact that you can speak English (or Japanese, Spanish, Hebrew or Hindi). Be grateful you have two eyes or a healthy heart or for the fact that you don't live in a war zone. And be grateful to others. Bless the farmer whose effort brought the fruit that's on your breakfast table. Bless the factory workers who put together the car you drive. Bless the cashier at the store where you buy your toothpaste. And bless the person who serves your food in the next restaurant you visit (this is life-changing stuff, even though it doesn't seem like it).

The attitude of gratitude. Counting your blessings. Not taking things for granted. I'll bet you have a lot more to be thankful for than you currently see. Just think about it. Just get grateful. Then fasten your seat belt. And watch what comes.

What you value in your life increases in value.

14

TAKE CHARGE FAST

Real leadership truly is about assuming personal responsibility. It's about creating rich results. It's about taking charge to get things done—whether you are on the front line or in the C-Suite. Here's what I mean.

Was buying groceries yesterday. Standing in line. Nothing moved. I looked ahead and saw a flustered woman—seemed her debit card didn't work. The cashier looked like a deer caught in headlights. He just froze. Didn't explain what was going on (I later learned the system went down). Didn't apologize to his customers for the delay. Didn't do anything to try to move things along. Just gave us a little fear-grin and started to whistle a nervous little whistle. Sounds so obvious, but it's true that leadership occurs in moments of challenge, not during moments of ease.

Leadership shows up when things at work—and in life—test us. Each of us, as a Leader Without Title, must rise to that challenge. We need to shine when things don't go as planned. And we have to take charge. Fast. Eventually, the system got back up, the debit card was put through and I moved through the line. But next time I'm at that grocery store and I have a choice, I'll find a cashier who gets it. Who thinks quickly. Who gets things done, when others just freeze.

Sounds so obvious, but it's true that leadership occurs in moments of challenge, not during moments of ease.

15

IDEAS ARE WORTHLESS

Controversial chapter title? Perhaps. But I think it's true. I've heard so many gurus say that ideas are the currency of success and thinking drives business and we become what we consider all day long. But, to me, ideation without execution is mere delusion (I dare you to share that line at your next team meeting). In other words, an idea, no matter how big, only assumes value when it's acted upon and brought to life.

This world of ours is full of great thinkers who never realized their greatness. They were strong on the thinking side but weak on the execution side. And they suffered as a result of that constraint. (German poet Johann von Goethe said, "Whatever you can do, or dream you can do, begin it. Boldness has genius, power and magic.") World-class people get both right. They are superb strategically and brilliant tactically. Really creative and really good at getting things done.

So jump-start your commitment around execution. Yes, capture your ideas and bask in the glow of a remarkably imaginative thought that has the power to improve how you work or the way you live. And then reach deep into yourself and have the discipline to do whatever it takes to make that idea a reality. Because nothing happens until you move.

This world of ours is full of great thinkers who never realized their greatness.

16

OPEN YOUR EYES

Just saw something that stunned me. I walked up to my favorite
Starbucks. Saw a car, engine running, baby in the back seat—and
no driver. The father had pulled up to the front of the store and
dashed in to get his morning java. Coffee over kid?

It's easy to get so caught up in the rush of busyness and the
call of our routines that we forget the imperative of being aware
of the very things we are doing. "Most men would rather die
than think," wrote philosopher Bertrand Russell ("Many do," he
added). Human beings are the only creatures in the world that can
step out of themselves and reflect on their thoughts and actions.
Monkeys can't do this. Dogs can't. Cats can't. Only we can.

If you can breathe oxygen today, then in my mind you have
the gift of being able to show leadership behavior over the coming
hours (and days/months/years). Leadership is about showing up
at your best. You know that. It's about being excellent amid changing times and celebrating the people around you. And leadership is
about being aware. Aware of your thoughts. Aware of your actions.
Aware of your mission. Aware of your priorities. Aware of your talents. Aware of your fears. Aware of your passions. Aware that time

is short. Aware of the brilliance presented to you by the life you get to lead (and yes, mine gets messy too).

So live with your eyes wide open. Clarity preceeds mastery. Think about things. Shine brighter than ever before. Act impeccably. And stand guard over babies in cars.

It's easy to get so caught up in the rush of busyness and the call of our routines that we forget the imperative of being aware of the very things we are doing.

17

SYMBOLS OF GLORY

Walking to school with the kids today. Breathtaking autumn morning here in my hometown. Fall colors, fresh air, crisp temperatures. My favorite time of the year.

Colby tells me that one of his buddies has a rubber turtle in his car. Said it reminds his parents to drive slowly and respect the lives of others on the road. Nice. Made me think about the importance of symbolic reminders—tokens we can strategically place at important places to help us remember what's most important. What matters. What we want to stand for.

One of the simplest tactics I suggest to clients at my leadership workshops is to put your three most important professional and personal commitments on a 3-inch × 5-inch card and post it on your bathroom mirror, so that you see them first thing in the morning. (I know it sounds cheesy, but it works.) This little practice affects your awareness. Radically. Your awareness then shapes your choices. And your choices shape your results. Extraordinary people are dramatically focused on their best To Do's. It's all they think, talk and dream about. (I recall reading about John Risley, founder of Clearwater Fine Foods—one of the world's largest seafood companies—who said, "When I want a deal, I think about nothing else but how to get it done. I wake up at night to use the bathroom, I'm thinking about the deal. I'm very focused.") And with that rare focus, they get to where they need to be. With fewer detours than the rest of us.

So what Symbols of Glory might you use to keep you in your finest form? What tokens of excellence can you find that will quickly help you get back to your priorities when the crush of daily events clamors for your attention? You deserve to live an extraordinary life. Start by finding your symbols—ones that represent the person you are ready to become.

What tokens of excellence can you find that will quickly help you get back to your priorities when the crush of daily events clamors for your attention?

18

BE UNREASONABLE

One of my favorite quotes comes from George Bernard Shaw, who noted, "The reasonable man adapts himself to the world; the unreasonable one persists in trying to adapt the world to himself. Therefore, all progress depends on the unreasonable man." Please think about that idea for a moment. I suggest it's a big one.

Sure, be practical and operate intelligently as you move through your world. I agree, it's important to use common sense. True, foolish risks can lead to difficult consequences. But having said that, don't be so scared of failure and disappointment that you fail to dream. Don't always be so reasonable and practical and sensible that you refuse to seize glorious opportunities when they show up. Push the envelope as to what's possible for you. Remember, critics have always laughed at the visions of bold thinkers and remarkable visionaries. Ignore them. And know that every outstanding piece of human progress was achieved through the heroic efforts of someone who was told their idea was impossible to realize. The world needs more dreamers. Unreasonable souls who fight the urge to be ordinary. Who resist the seduction of complacency and doing things the way they have always been done. You can be one of them. Beginning today.

Kahlil Gibran, in *The Prophet*, made the point far more beautifully than I ever could, when he wrote, "The lust for comfort murders the passion of the soul."

Remember, critics have always laughed at the visions of bold thinkers and remarkable visionaries. Ignore them.

19

NOT ALL LEADERS ARE THE SAME

Many executives come up to me after presentations and ask me about my statement "Everyone's a leader." I've observed that the best companies on the planet have one trait in common: They grow leaders throughout the organization faster than their competition. Making that happen is their number-one focus. And they do it fast.

But I'm not saying everyone should run the company. That makes no sense. Everyone can show leadership behavior but that doesn't mean everyone will lead the organization. Here's a metaphor that I hope will make this distinction clearer.

I love U2. Bono is the lead singer. Larry Mullen, Jr., is the drummer. Chaos would ensue if Larry tried to be the lead singer and Bono got confused and played the drums. Or imagine the tour manager thinking he could be Bono for a night and walking out on stage to do so while Bono was in his dressing room. Not good.

Know your role. Everyone needs to behave like a leader— no matter what they do. That means that everyone needs to take responsibility for generating the superb results for which they are accountable. Everyone needs to do their part to shape culture.

Everyone needs to be positive and inspirational. Everyone needs to go the extra mile for customers—and view change as an opportunity to make things better. Everyone really can be a leader and have a profound impact by standing for excellence within the area of their responsibility. But not everyone is the same.

Everyone can show leadership behavior but that doesn't mean everyone will lead the organization.

20

I LEARN FROM MY MISTAKES (sometimes)

There's nothing wrong with making a mistake. We are human. Mistakes offer us a powerful way to learn and grow. Just don't make the same mistake more than once. That shows you're resisting the lesson available to you. Suggests you're not listening to life. Shows you're not paying attention.

In *The Greatness Guide*, I wrote about how I missed a window of opportunity to meet Harvey Keitel in a Toronto hotel lobby. Just didn't seize what Carlos Castaneda called "the cubic centimeter of chance" that presented itself. But I vowed to make amends. I promised you I would. Well, I kept my word. Was downtown for meetings with my publisher. Was having a quick sushi lunch at my favorite Japanese restaurant. Guess who was sitting at the next table? Eric Clapton. Seriously.

When the time was right (the time to seize an opportunity will never be ideal, but I let the man finish his tempura), I said hello. Sure my pulse quickened (you know I'm a very ordinary person). And yes, I worried about rejection. *But if you don't try, you'll never know.* I realized that if I took the leap, I had a chance to meet him. But that if I didn't, I'd be sure that I never would.

So I did. We ended up having a nice chat. Interesting person. Another conversation that somehow will shape me—as every conversation does.

Each day life sends you chances to learn, grow and step into your best. Don't miss them. Some opportunities never come again. Regret is a choice.

If you don't try, you'll never know.

21

ASK POWERFUL QUESTIONS

One of the fastest ways to find the solution to an issue or challenge you are facing is to ask the right question. The right question inevitably leads you to the correct answer. Questions matter. In business, remarkable performers are dazzlingly good at getting to the right question. The one that speeds them to the place they need to reach and offers them the missing piece they need to find. And in life, asking yourself a powerful question will allow you to step into a whole new set of possibilities that you may have missed while you were locked into an old way of seeing things. Like the lesson amid a so-called failure. Or the opportunity that inhabits a setback.

Here are six questions that I share with the clients with whom we do leadership development work. I suggest you write them down and then find some time today to answer them in your journal.

- *What one thing—if I did it—would profoundly improve the way I work (and how I live)?*
- *What needs to happen between now and the end of the next 90 days for me to feel that this is the best quarter of my work and personal life? (Remember, clarity preceeds mastery.)*

- *Who do I need to express appreciation to? (Make your list long.)*
- *What would I like to improve, professionally and personally?*
- *What could I be grateful for that I'm currently not grateful for?*
- *How do I want to be remembered at my retirement party?*

And as you make this day extraordinary, I'll leave you with one of my favorite quotes (which comes from Mark Twain): "If everyone was satisfied with themselves, there would be no heroes."

In business, remarkable performers are dazzlingly good at getting to the right question, the one that speeds them to the place they need to reach.

22

BE BREATHTAKINGLY HUMBLE

It's 4:15 a.m. (best time of the day). I'm drinking a perfect cup of coffee. Listening to Simple Plan's song "Perfect World." Thinking. About life, learning. And authentic excellence. Powerful thought I want to share with you: The humblest is the greatest.

Canada's richest man, Kenneth Thomson, died a while ago. *The Globe and Mail*, one of Canada's national newspapers, published a profile on him titled "A Billionaire's Breakfast." Thomson's brunch ritual was described: ". . . meals didn't come with a side of caviar . . . every weekend he would stroll into (a small local) restaurant and order a brunch buffet for $10.95." Love it.

In an interview, the restaurant owner spoke of Thomson's extraordinary humility and noted, "He was always so gracious, but simple. He joked with the staff and never let on who he was." He always got his own food from the buffet table, smiled when he entered and, last Christmas, even took the time to take a photo with all the staff, which he then had developed, later returning to the restaurant with a copy for each staff member. "Now everyone has something to remember him by."

Something to remember him by. Unforgettable words. Humility. An essential element in the creation of a beautiful legacy.

*Humility. An essential element in the
creation of a beautiful legacy.*

23

BE A COOL BRAND

You are a brand. No matter what you think, when people hear your name, they conjure up some association. When people see you, an emotional response gets evoked. Like it or not, you (and your reputation) truly are a brand. So I gently suggest that you manage it. Well. Actually, what I really want to challenge you to do is to take the steps you need to take to become a cool brand. One that shouts "cutting edge," "with it," "original" and "revolutionary."

Cool brands that immediately come to mind for me include Apple, Virgin, Phat Farm and Prada. They are fresh and hip and stylish. They *get* it. And they stand out in a world that loves conformity. They make me go "wow." You could do the same—for yourself.

What would it take for you to become a cool brand? So that when people think of you, words like *innovative* or *world class* or *unique* infuse their minds. What would it take for you to become the Steve Jobs of your team or the Salvador Dali of your workplace or the Russell Simmons of your division? How could you become so strikingly great at what you do and who you are that everyone around you adores everything about you? Something to consider. Something to act on.

What would it take for you to become the Steve Jobs of your team or the Salvador Dalí of your workplace or the Russell Simmons of your division?

24

CHERISH CONFLICT

Everybody runs from conflict. It makes us feel bad, so we avoid it. Hope it will somehow resolve itself. It never does. Instead it just festers like a bad wound (what we resist really does persist).

Here's my take on conflict: Conflict is nothing more than an opportunity for greater growth and a deeper personal connection. Every conflict carries within it a chance for you to learn a powerful lesson and to grow as a human being (in your understanding and awareness and perspective). And every conflict, whether with a loved one or a customer, is a gorgeous opportunity to forge an even closer bond with them. By turning their dissatisfaction into a wow for both of you.

So don't run from conflict. Don't send the email when you know you need to speak some truth face to face. Leadership is about balancing compassion *with courage*. And though it can feel so messy, in truth it's a gift. Embrace it. Relish the potential it carries. Celebrate it. It can serve you so well.

Here's my take on conflict:
Conflict is nothing more than an
opportunity for greater growth
and a deeper connection.

25

THE RESPONSIBILITY METER

Imagine a dashboard with a meter on it. At one end is the word FREEDOM. At the other, the word RESPONSIBILITY. To me, being a leader and living a remarkable life means striking the delicate balance between the two. In other words, the needle on your Responsibility Meter should stay in the middle. Ideally.

Life's all about balance. And one of the most vital of all balance points is the one involving freedom and responsibility. Yes, be free. Enjoy the moment. Be wildly passionate. Have a fabulous time. Live in the now. And yet, be responsible. Set your goals. Keep your promises. Get important things done. Fulfill your duties.

Where does your life—this very minute—register on the Responsibility Meter? Too much time enjoying your freedom and not enough time doing what's required to build a world-class career and world-class days? Or the other way around? Being at either extreme means being out of balance. So here's an excellent idea: Think about what being at the middle of the meter would look like. Because better awareness drives better choices. And better choices create better results.

Life's all about balance. And one of the most vital of all balance points is the one involving freedom and responsibility.

26

A LUST FOR GROWTH

Just read a quote that provoked me: "Growth is the only evidence of life." Intelligent words. They come from John Henry Newman. You know I adore the whole notion of growth. I believe that's why we are here. To grow and expand through the work we do, the actions we take and the lives we lead (please remember: Don't just live your life, lead it). Growth matters. It's what ultimately makes us feel fulfilled (we are happiest when we are growing, and realizing our potential). Growth energizes us (even when it's uncomfortable—and most growth is). Makes us who we truly are.

What comes to mind when you think about your best teacher or mentor or boss? Good thoughts, right? You appreciate the lessons and learning and growth that that human being promoted in you. So why would you feel any differently about the most trying/challenging/frustrating events of your life? Are those not the very events that have most shaped you? And evoked your best and highest? Taught you what you needed to learn to get you to where you stand today? They too were your teachers. They too championed your personal expansion. They too inspired your growth. So honor them. Because they have helped you more than you know.

I adore the whole notion of growth.
I believe that's why we are here.

27

CREDIT DOESN'T MATTER

"You can accomplish anything in life, provided that you do not mind who gets the credit," observed Harry Truman. Splendid thought. Leave your ego at the front door when you go to work today and just do superb work. Good things will happen. For you.

It's so human to crave applause and recognition and acclaim. We all want to be appreciated by our peers and revered by the tribe. But leadership is about a lot more than trying to look good in the eyes of others. It's about standing for a Cause (as Pablo Picasso added, "It's your Work in life that is the ultimate seduction"). It's about being BIW (Best in the World) at what you do. It's about leaving people better than you found them. And it's about not worrying who gets the credit for a job well done.

People who are outstanding always get found out. The cliché is true: The cream always rises to the top. The best always come to light. And the Great Ones among us can never be held back.

"You can accomplish anything in life, provided that you do not mind who gets the credit," observed Harry Truman.

28

THE BRILLIANCE OF ACCEPTANCE

I'm reading a book by my dear friend Richard Carlson, author of *Don't Sweat the Small Stuff*, who sadly passed away a while ago. The book's called *Don't Get Scrooged*, and I just finished the chapter "Acceptance: The Ultimate Solution." Made me stop. And think.

Richard writes, "Acceptance may sound like inaction, but when you try to practice it, you'll see that it is anything but doing nothing. It sometimes requires more effort than the complaining, confronting or clamming up you would normally do. But . . . once you experience the freedom it brings—acceptance can become almost second nature."

Acceptance. Looking for the blessing in disguise amid adversity. Relaxing into whatever situation you find yourself in. Embracing the age-old adage that life doesn't give you what you want but just might send you what you need (thanks again, Mick). We all get hard days and mean seasons, from time to time. That's because you and I are enrolled in Greatness School. And challenge, conflict, confusion and uncertainty are beautifully orchestrated vehicles for our growth. But days do get better and seasons always change. By accepting "what is," the bitter times will be shorter and your gorgeous days will get longer. And that's my highest wish for you. Always.

We all get hard days and mean seasons, from time to time. That's because you and I are enrolled in Greatness School.

29

BE A BEAUTIFUL THINKER

I'm sitting in my hotel room in Karachi as I write this. An absolutely fascinating city. The sounds. The culture. The people. All a wonderful education for me. I'm grateful to be here.

Reading Jhumpa Lahiri's *The Namesake*. Beautifully written. It prompted an idea: Become a Beautiful Thinker. Commit to making each of your thoughts a thing of beauty. Devote yourself to coming up with stunning insights and ideas and reflections that are outright masterpieces. You've heard it a hundred times in as many different ways: You become what you think about. And the thoughts you use become self-fulfilling prophecies. Expect extraordinary things to unfold for you, and they will. The motivators say it. The teachers say it. The sages say it. Ever wonder why?

I think I finally understand why the idea is accurate. It's not some esoteric philosophy. It's simple logic. Here we go: The actions you take each day create the results of your life. And since every action you take has been preceded by a thought (thinking truly is the ancestor of performance), what you focus on does drive your reality. British Prime Minister Benjamin Disraeli said it so well when he wrote, "You will never go any higher than your thinking." As a human being you will never act in a way bigger than your thoughts. Dream big and your behavior will follow. Think small and you'll play small.

This concept cascades through every dimension of our lives. Think people are good and you walk through your days with an open heart. And that very behavior actually creates your reality, because people *do good things for good people*. Think you deserve the best and your actions will reflect that confidence. Better actions will then drive better results. Expect to be world class in your career or within your community and that brilliant thinking will shape the way you work as well as the way you live. And that exceptional conduct will drive exceptional outcomes.

I hope I have been able to express this point clearly. Because I believe it's a big one that is too easy to neglect. Your thoughts do shape your reality. Your thinking does form your world. What you focus on truly will expand. And what you dwell upon will most definitely determine your destiny.

Commit to making each of your
thoughts a thing of beauty.

30

OPINIONS DON'T MATTER

It doesn't matter what other people think of you. All that matters is what *you* think of you. We waste so much energy worrying about the opinions of others, wanting to be liked, needing to please. But authentic leadership and real personal mastery are all about rising above social approval—to self-approval. Respect you. So long as you are living by your values, being authentic, running your own race and doing your dreams, why worry what anyone else thinks or feels or says about you? Success isn't a popularity contest. And at the end of each day, what matters most is whether you were true to yourself.

Success isn't a popularity contest.

31

ARE YOU JOKEABLE?

Bianca, my 11-year-old daughter, is a wise, wonderful and hilarious kid. She wants to be the drummer for Green Day when she grows up. She loves her dog, Max. And when Bianca laughs, the whole world laughs with her. Loudly.

So we are having a great conversation (I spend a lot of time just talking with my kids; I never have my BlackBerry on when I'm with them). She tells me the boys in her class think she's cool. They love making her laugh. They get that she's got a big spirit. Then she shares a line that cracks me up: "Dad, all my friends say I'm jokeable."

So let me ask you a question: How jokeable are you? When was the last time you allowed someone to make you laugh so hard tears streamed down your cheeks? How often do you sit back and giggle at life—even at the messy stuff? (Life's messy at times, isn't it; love the messes—your richest growth resides in them.) The best among us don't take themselves too seriously (no one will take you seriously if you take yourself too seriously). They do their best and then let go, letting life do the rest. Life has its own intelligence.

So be jokeable. Relax. Yes, go for world class. But blend that drive with a sense of amusement and festivity. Hold on to life with a loose grip. Every setback carries the seeds of an even greater opportunity (it's taken me about 43 years to get that one). And life was never meant to be an ordeal. It was meant to be pure joy.

When was the last time you allowed someone to make you laugh so hard tears streamed down your cheeks?

32

HOW TO GET POWER

Here's a simple truth I've learned from the best leaders I've worked with as a success coach, professional speaker and leadership consultant: The only way to truly get power is to give it away. The more you rely on, trust and believe in your team and the bigger the investment you make in getting them to their greatness, the larger will be the commitment, engagement and outright devotion they have toward you.

Power doesn't come from forcing people to listen to you and coercing them to do what you say because you have the right title on your business card. Nope. Real power comes when you spread your passion, offer people a reason to climb your strategic mountaintops, treat them with rare respect and give them permission to shine, grow and Lead Without Title. Be there for people and they'll be there for you. Simple stuff, but as I mentioned earlier, I'm a pretty simple guy.

Here's a great line from Richard Kovacevich, CEO of Wells Fargo (I had to read it a few times to get it): "It's the best five players that win the game, not the five best players."

The only way to truly get power
is to give it away.

33

HABITS ARE HIP

Okay, so maybe habits aren't the hippest thing in the world. But they just might be the most important. What separates the best from the rest comes down to habits. A few good ones (that's really all it takes—two or three really good ones) will make a massive difference in the way your career and your life looks at the end. They will make the difference between mediocrity and mastery. So choose them well.

Here's a metaphor that may serve nicely to make my point: A good habit is like a sturdy oak tree. It starts off as a little seed, planted in a single moment. Fail to nurture it daily and it dies a fast death. But tend to it, just a bit each day, and the thing grows. Until one day it's so strong that it is next to impossible to break.

Your habits will define how close to your personal mountaintop you get. Ones I've observed in world-class people include the following:

- *Align all your actions with the highest levels of excellence and integrity*
- *Put relationships with people first*

- *Leverage adversity to make you/your career and your life even better.*
- *Get up early.*
- *Under-promise and over-deliver
  (always give people more than they expect and you'll win).*
- *Be a passionate learner (read daily, listen to audio programs by
  insightful thinkers and attend seminars).*
- *Spend the first 60 minutes of each day dreaming, planning or
  simply working out to maintain remarkable personal vitality.*
- *Balance being tremendously good at what you do with becoming
  a tremendously interesting and well-rounded human being.*

Just a few to pick from. To get you going. To plant your seeds.

What separates the best from the rest comes down to habits.

34

FIND PERFECT MOMENTS

I had a Perfect Moment today. It wasn't a standing ovation in front of a thousand people. It wasn't a phone call from a publisher sharing some good news. It wasn't a Fortune 500 company calling to book a leadership presentation or coaching engagement for their team. No, it was a far more important thing that occurred in my life on this morning. And it was incredibly basic (as are the best things in life).

As I got out of my car in the parking lot of our office, I noticed an amazing fragrance in the air. It was pure beauty. So sweet and breathtaking. I looked around and saw that I'd parked under a tree overflowing with red and pink blossoms. Spring had sprung, and the tree was spreading its magic. I just stood there. Closed my eyes, entranced by the smell. And the moment. I felt grateful to be alive. Sure, I have challenges I'm dealing with (the only ones who don't are dead). Sure, life could always be better. But happiness is all about gaining a sense of proportion and perspective. And we all have many blessings in our lives, like people who love us or work that gives our days meaning or healthy kids or simple gifts like food on the table and two eyes to see through. Like the Perfect Moment in the parking lot.

Life is so very short. Yes, it's important to focus on excellence in your career and arriving at splendid success, however you define it. I totally agree with that. But equally important is enjoying the ride. Laughing. Having fun. Experiencing adventure. And not missing out on Perfect Moments. Mostly, they are free. And they are right in front of you. Today. If only you make the time to look for them.

Sure, life could always be better.
But happiness is all about gaining a sense
of proportion and perspective.

35

THE PARADOX OF PRAISE

I was driving Colby to school and got an idea I want to share with you. We were talking about *Everybody Loves Raymond*, the television show my kids adore. In particular, we discussed the tension between Raymond's (cranky) mother, Marie, and Ray's (loving) wife, Deborah. Colby said they don't like each other because Marie doesn't like Deborah's cooking. I asked him to go deeper and to figure out the real issue. After we discussed it for a while, we both heard the coin drop: We got that the real reason Marie doesn't like Deborah is that she feels threatened by the love between Deborah and her son Raymond. She's insecure. Thinks she might lose him. So she's hard on Deborah and has no praise for her. Ever.

Made me think about praise within the workplace (and within the home). A rare commodity. Praise, to me, is like the sun: The more you give away, the more everything around you grows toward you. However, most people don't give praise freely (even though it's free). According to a Gallup Organization survey, the number-one reason employees leave an organization is that they don't feel appreciated by their supervisor. Yet, most managers give away neither praise nor appreciation. Because they think it makes them look inferior.

Here is the truth as far as I can tell: Giving praise to all those around you, when they most deserve it, makes you look like more. It elevates you. It makes you look like a hero. It makes you look like a giant within the workplace. To everyone around you. So don't withhold what your teammates most crave. We all want to feel special. I do. You do. And so does Deborah.

Giving praise to all those around you, when they most deserve it, makes you look like more. It elevates you. It makes you look like a hero.

36

LUCK VERSUS LAW

It's true what they say: The harder you work, the luckier you get.
You may wonder, "Is a remarkable life the result of luck or are
there a series of natural laws at play that produce great results
once we align ourselves with them?" Well here's my answer. Good
things happen to people who do good things. Do the right things
and you cannot help but see the right results.

I've been thinking a lot lately about farming. No, I don't plan
on giving up this leadership and personal success stuff and spending
my days planting corn (though it would be a cool way to live). But
just think about it: The laws of the farm and the laws of nature are
the same laws that rule our business and personal lives. As you sow,
so shall you reap. Care for and nurture your farm and a bountiful
harvest cannot help but develop. Care for and nurture your career
or your health or your relationships and do you really believe that
you will be denied an abundance of produce? Not possible.

Sure, sometimes we get lucky. That's just icing on the cake.
To me, a rare-air life is the result of living in alignment with the
laws of nature. Doing things like adding value to your customers
and all those who surround you. Treating everyone you meet like

a VIP. Being unexpectedly honest and surprisingly enthusiastic. Just keep doing these things and you'll be fine. And remember, the more seeds you plant, the more plants you'll see.

Good things happen to people who do good things. Do the right things and you cannot help but see the right results.

37

CAMEL'S BACK SYNDROME

Most organizations don't fall apart as a result of one big blow. Most relationships don't end because of one grand argument. Most lives don't fall to pieces due to one sad event. No, I suggest to you that sustained failure happens as the consequence of small, daily acts of neglect that stack up over time to lead to a blowup, and a breakdown.

Remember the camel's back metaphor. Pieces of straw kept getting piled on the poor animal. Each piece alone was light and caused little harm. But piece after piece got placed on the camel's back until eventually the load was so heavy that a single added straw broke his back.

I call this Camel's Back Syndrome. A little neglect inevitably leads to businesses and lives of striking disrepair. The best truly do sweat the minor details. They get the seemingly insignificant things right. They have the discipline to shine at the tiny projects and activities and To Do's, which give birth to the spectacularly big ones. They understand that lasting success comes via evolution, not revolution. And so can you.

Sustained failure happens as the consequence of small, daily acts of neglect that stack up over time to lead to a blowup, and a breakdown.

38

BURN THE EXTRA 1 PERCENT

Reading British *GQ* on a flight home from Rome. (Rome's fantastic. As an Aussie friend said to me recently, "You can take any turn and discover a history lesson.") The biggest idea I ran across in the magazine comes from Chris Carmichael, the coach of seven-time Tour de France–winner Lance Armstrong who said, "The last 1 percent most people keep in reserve is the extra percent champions have the courage to burn." Magnificent thought. I hope we never forget it.

Spend every bit of your energy playing at your best and creating world-class results. Offer every bit of your potential to all you do. And awaken your talents. And your inner fire. So at the end, you can say, "I gave it my all. I did my best." That would be fantastic. Wouldn't it? And please remember—the opportunity for outright greatness comes at the very moment that ordinary people give up.

"The last 1 percent most people keep in reserve is the extra percent champions have the courage to burn."

39

REMEMBER RECIPROCITY

It's only human nature to want to help those who've helped us. Each of us has a deep-seated hunger to do unto others as they've done unto us. And so I do believe that we get back what we give out. An example.

I just drove 20 minutes out of my way to buy gas. Why would I do that when I have a big list of To Do's and a full schedule for today? Why would I do such an inconvenient thing when convenience suggests that I go to the station two minutes away from my office? Answer: I did it because I wanted to return a favor. To someone who was good to me. To a good person.

A few weeks ago, after dropping the kids off at school I noticed I had a flat tire. I went to three gas stations, and only one could fix my tire quickly. An elderly gentleman in overalls with the name Tony stitched over his heart said he'd be happy to help me. Offered me a coffee while I waited. Entertained me while he did the repair. He did his work with obvious joy. A Leader Without Title. People like him inspire me. Make me want to be a better man.

So I've been looking for an opportunity to show my appreciation. It starts today, by giving him my business. And then I'll be sending my friends over. And they'll tell others and so on. Because Tony deserves to win. And I want to reciprocate.

It's only human nature to want to help those who've helped us. Each of us has a deep-seated hunger to do unto others as they've done unto us.

40

SAY WHAT YOU MEAN

Ever notice that it's the people we love most that we take most for granted? Odd, isn't it. It's easy to spend less time with your family because they will always be there for you (or so you assume). It's easy to put off expressing your love to your loved ones because there seems to be no urgency to do so. It's easy to let home relationships slip because you assume there are more pressing things to deal with. But what could possibly be more important than your family? What's the point of being über-successful, but alone? A full family photo album is far more impressive to me than an overflowing bank account. Honestly.

So pick up the phone and tell your parents that you love them. Before you leave for work, give your spouse a kiss—like you really mean it. And please, hug your kids and tell them that you adore them. Your kids will only be young once. And when that window of opportunity closes, it will close forever.

It's the people we love most
that we take most for granted.

41

RICHARD BRANSON
AND OUTRAGEOUS OPTIMISM

Just finished an issue of *Fortune*. One article described a tech conference held on Necker Island, the Caribbean hideaway Richard Branson bought 25 years ago. Of the young Net geniuses in attendance and their visionary insights. Of the fun had by all as they sailed and drank great wine and engaged in powerful conversations (each of us need to inject "powerful conversations" into our weeks to energize, elevate and sustain us). And then it came down to Branson, founder of the Virgin conglomerate. The writer, David Kirkpatrick, noted that Branson can speak to anyone about almost anything, from food to sports. But what struck him most about the man was his infectious good cheer. Branson seemed to be in good spirits all the time. A News Corp executive agreed and added, "That's something I've noticed about these moguls. They're almost always the most optimistic people in the room." Interesting.

So our takeaway is that optimism isn't superficial or soft or boring. Nope. It's a mission-critical tool for anyone devoted to getting to authentic excellence—and a life fully lived. Every day brings challenges to those who dare and risk and dream. That's just part of the game when you are devoted to being great. Being the most optimistic person in the room will help you transcend the rest. And get to where you've always wanted to be.

Being the most optimistic person in the room will help you transcend the rest.

42

BEWARE OF VICTIMSPEAK

Back to a theme I shared with you in *The Greatness Guide*: the power of words. Words shape the way you feel. They influence the way you process reality. And they can either take you closer to your mountaintop or draw you nearer to the valley. Use world-class words and you'll get to your world-class life.

I was in a Starbucks in Manhattan yesterday. The guy in front of me ordered a chai latte. The barista said she was out of chai. He looked wounded. Seriously. I wish you could have seen his face. Like he just got an arrow through the heart. His reply? Classic victimspeak: "How could you do this to me?" I waited for his smile. It never came.

No matter what life sends us, we are responsible for the way we respond. We truly are. We can own our reaction. We can choose what we do with the situation. We can be bitter, or show up better. Tons of choices—at *all* times. Starting with our words. Choose them well. Leaders do.

No matter what life sends us,
we are responsible for the way we respond.

43

I'M STRETCHING TOO

I know I encourage you to push the envelope. To innovate. To elevate. To step up to the next level with the work you do and within the life you have the privilege to lead. And I know I talk a lot about running to your fears (remember that most of the stuff we are afraid of never even comes close to happening) and hugging your discomfort. Well, I do my best to do the same. Here's an example.

I just spent two days last week in a recording studio. For a long time I've had the dream of making music with a powerful message. I used to play guitar in a rock band in law school (poorly yet passionately) and I needed to get back to that love. And you know this: There will never be the ideal time to do the dreams in your heart. So I took a risk. (Al Pacino recently told Larry King, "You will only be as good as the chances you take.") I reached out to the two amazing partners at the Orange Record Label and shared my vision. Guess what, "no ask, no get." They signed me to a deal. Immediately.

These past two days found me in a studio with some of the most creative people I've ever met. Writers and musicians. Visionaries and dreamers. All banded together to help me create brilliant music that will inspire people to make their lives extraordinary. Genuine works of art. I had to sing (stop laughing). I had to play guitar. I had to let go of my safe harbor and be a beginner again. "How was it?" you ask. Breathtakingly great. (If you want to see me playing, watch the CNN clip at robinsharma.com.) I was scared, excited, joy-filled and delighted. I trembled. And I laughed. It was an experience I'll never forget—one that is part of the personal story I call life. So get out there. Risk. Ask. Dream. Dare. Fall. Fail. And never let anyone tell you that your dreams can't come true. Eventually someone's going to do what you dream of doing. Why not you?

Never let anyone tell you that your dreams can't come true. Eventually someone's going to do what you dream of doing. Why not you?

44

STOP TRYING SO HARD

One of the core organizing principles of my life is that success is the result of a delicate balance between making things happen and letting things happen. Yes, we have the responsibility to set our goals and realize our potential and play at our very best. We need to do our part. Good things definitely unfold for people who are devoted to doing great things. But I suggest we also need to show a gentle commitment to letting things unfold. In other words, do your best—then let life do the rest.

Life will always lead you to a place that's better (even when it may not seem like it). I've learned it is important to let life lead you (not an easy lesson to get—I know; still working on that one myself). If you've tried everything possible to realize an outcome and it just hasn't worked out as planned, stop trying so hard. Relax. Maybe nothing's wrong. Maybe the timing's not right. Maybe what you wanted wasn't in your best interests. Maybe while one door seems to be closing, another is actually opening. And often, once you let go of what you thought was best, space is created for something even better to arrive. Because every ending ushers in a brand-new beginning.

*Life will always lead you to
a place that's better.*

45

THE MIRROR TEST

I believe it's important to remember that when you know better, you can do better. With higher levels of awareness, you can make smarter choices. And the more clarity you get as to who you want to become, the more quickly you can start making the choices needed to get you there. Clarity really does offer a framework for more intelligent decision-making (and we become our decisions).

Here's a simple tool for you: the Mirror Test. Look into the mirror and ask yourself the following question: "What one thing could I do today that if I did it, my professional and personal life would get to its NLG: Next Level of Greatness?" Then think about that one thing. Reflect on executing that step superbly. And go out and do it. Act with courage. Now. Remember, small daily improvements lead over time to stunning results.

Ask yourself the following question:
"What one thing could I do today that
if I did it, my professional and personal
life would get to its NLG:
Next Level of Greatness?"

46

FIND UNCOMFORTABLE FRIENDS

Okay, this one might challenge, provoke and even irritate you a bit (if so, I've done my job). Because we grow through ideas and experiences that stretch us. And all I want to do is help you grow (into your greatness).

The idea centers on the importance of surrounding yourself with people who cause you to leave the SHK: Safe Harbor of the Known. Why spend time with people at work who play at mediocre? Why have friends in your personal life who resign themselves to being ordinary? We really do become who we drink coffee with. We really will become our associations.

Powerful thought: You will become a lot like the five people you spend most of your time with (hope I didn't scare you). So my suggestion is that you invite people into your professional and personal life who inspire you. Who will uplift you. Who will make you more extraordinary/authentic/unforgettable (and loving). Who are viscerally committed to world class. And, most importantly, who see the world through a different set of eyes. They'll challenge you. They'll push you. And sometimes maybe they'll even irritate you (if so, fantastic). This practice will serve you well. So that you grow. And reach. And evolve. So that you will never be the same.

Why spend time with people at work who play at mediocre? Why have friends in your personal life who resign themselves to being ordinary?

47

INNOVATE WHERE YOU ARE

To get to world class, it is absolutely essential to become an excellent innovator. Relentlessly making things better and passionately discovering new ways to add value, work smarter and move faster are core creative traits that the best in business live by. And to be astonishingly creative and generate those big ideas that catapult you to your highest level, you don't need to go walking in the woods or find some sanctuary. Some of the best insights come from innovating and thinking outside of the box at the very place where you now stand. As Tom Kelley, president of the Silicon Valley–based design firm IDEO, observed, "Brainstorming at ski lodges and beach resorts can be counterproductive. Do you want your team members to think that creativity and inspiration can only happen at high altitudes or within walking distance from an ocean? Don't get me wrong: Off-sites are fine. But remember, you want the buzz of creativity to blow through your offices as regularly as a breeze at the beach." So perfectly said.

*To get to world class, it is absolutely
essential to become an excellent innovator.*

48

PRIDE IN PARENTING

Leadership begins at home. Your family is an organization that needs to be managed, cherished and elevated if you aim to truly get to the rare air life I believe you deserve. I also believe that the highest moments of our lives are the moments shared with those we love.

I just dropped Bianca off at school. Saw a car with a fantastic license plate. It said simply, RKIDSROC. Made me smile.

How proud are you of your kids? Are they your primary priority? Mine definitely are. I'd let go of all I'm doing in my work life in a second, if my children needed me to. Do you spend quantity time with your kids as well as quality time? I've been a father for 13 years now and I must share with you that no matter what toys, video games or gifts I give my gang, nothing beats my time. That's all they really want. That's all they've ever really wanted. As I wrote in *The Greatness Guide*, I can't tell you how many über-rich executive coaching clients have flown their jets to meet me in Toronto, sat down with me and shared that though they "have it all," they have nothing. Because they missed their kids' childhoods. Money is not the most important form of wealth. It just isn't.

So today, love your loved ones. Cherish them. And tell them all the things you've wanted to say but haven't had the courage to. You'll never regret showing them how proud you are of them. Ever.

Money is not the most important form of wealth.

49

THE HIDDEN MACHINERY

I recently read a fascinating issue of *Time*. All about the 100 Most Influential People in the World. Jobs is in there. So are Branson and Gore. Mittal makes the cut, as does Oprah. But one of the profiles that intrigued me most is the one on Leonardo DiCaprio. Because of a single turn of phrase used by filmmaker Martin Scorsese. He describes the first time he saw DiCaprio acting: "In his performance, I didn't see the machinery." I had to put down the magazine after I read those words.

Masters make everything look so simple. The most brilliant of the best do their craft with effortless ease and exceptional grace, or at least, make it look that way to you and me. We can't see the machinery. We don't see all the early mornings and late nights spent working hard to be BIW (Best in the World). We don't observe the fierce determination that was invested to overcome impossible odds and make the dream come true. And we don't hear the laughter of the critics that needed to be ignored to get to the mountaintop. Remarkable performers—in entertainment, business, politics, education—all make it look easy. But it wasn't. It can take years to become an overnight sensation. Let's not forget that.

Masters make everything look so simple.
The most brilliant of the best do their craft
with effortless ease and exceptional grace,
or at least, make it look that way to
you and me.

50

DON'T WAIT FOR CHANGE

You know I've never claimed to be perfect. I've always maintained that I'm no guru and most definitely a work in progress. Very ordinary. I have my strengths. And my flaws (like every human being). One of my weaknesses is impatience. I just have this aching need to get great things done. Can't stand slow change. Need to make my impact, and to spend my talents (we all have them). Now.

Like some weaknesses, it's also a great source of success. I move things forward fast. Just love speed. Only results matter (I'm generalizing, a bit). Makes me think of what Clint Eastwood said in a recent issue of *Best Life*: "Sometimes if you want to see a change for the better, you have to take things into your own hands." Exactly.

Sure, work with your team. Yes, collaborate. Of course delegate to others who have strengths where you don't. But sometimes, when everyone else is waiting for someone else to take the first step, *you need to be the one to drive the change*. To me, that's courage in action. To me, that's using your life well. To me, that's leadership—and standing for being extraordinary.

Sometimes, when everyone else is waiting for someone else to take the first step, you need to be the one to drive the change.

51

FIRST PRINCIPLES FOR GREAT RELATIONSHIPS

The quality of your life comes down to the quality of your relationships. With your customers, with your suppliers, with your loved ones, with your self (big idea there). Commit to insanely great relationships and you'll have an insanely great life. And being a great human connector is pretty easy stuff. Remember, success is all about a masterful consistency around fundamentals.

The following seven First Principles are profoundly simple and yet simply profound—and isn't that the case for all great truths?

- *Be the first one to say hello (or* Namaste/Shalom/Hola/Salam Malekam, *or whatever may be appropriate) when you encounter another person. In other words, be kind first (which takes courage, because we're all scared of rejection).*
- *Smile a lot. It's one of the best ways to have someone open up to you. Remember, we make lasting impressions on people within the first few minutes of meeting them.*
- *Use people's names. This is really important. It shows that you care, and is a mark of respect.*
- *Look people in the eye when you speak to them.*

- *Become a world-class listener. Get this one right and you'll own the title of "Relationship Superstar." Most people don't listen. Most people are so self-focused that they fail to ask good questions when they meet another person. Listening and asking questions shows humility. It shows you are interested. It demonstrates that you are engaged—and not in love with yourself. Most people's idea of listening is waiting until the other person has finished speaking so that they can interject.*
- *Offer sincere compliments. Praise is free. Never miss an opportunity to celebrate and elevate another person, whether at work or at home. You'll connect with the best within them. And then they'll give you their best. Leave people feeling better than you found them.*
- *Treat everyone like royalty (and I do mean everyone; it scares me when someone's really nice to me but rude to a waiter—no consistency there). Behave as if you'll never see them again. When I get home from work each day, my kids come flying around the corner and hug me. Every day. Makes me feel like a king.*

Sure the above seven ideas are simple. Master these First Principles and you'll get to your mountaintop more quickly than you can imagine. *Greatness comes from mastery around the fundamentals.*

Never miss an opportunity to celebrate and elevate another person

---

52

WORRY VERSUS REFLECTION

So many thought leaders counsel us to avoid living in the past. "Live in the now," they advise. "Enjoy the moment." "The past is a grave." Well, I get what they are saying. But isn't there something good about going back and delighting in the delicious moments of the journey so far? And in learning from all we've experienced?

Which brings me to worry versus reflection. Whether you should revisit the past, to my mind, depends on your intention. If your intention in and reason for going back into your past is to dwell on bad experiences and to worry over things you cannot change and to rehash painful times, then I suggest it's an unhealthy act (a complete waste of time, actually; just keeps you stuck). But, if your intention is to reflect on the lessons that events have taught you and to grow in wisdom and to savor the precious memories that you were blessed enough to experience, well, then I think that's a good thing. Because you are letting your past serve *you*. And make you better.

I guess what I'm inviting you to consider is that it's a waste of time to fret over and regret things you've done that cannot be changed. But it's an intelligent use of time to bask in the good times, feel gratitude for them and use even the challenging times of your personal history to leverage your future success.

But isn't there something good about going back and delighting in the delicious moments of the journey so far? And in learning from all we've experienced?

53

BELIEVE IN OTHERS

I took my kids to see Hilary Swank's movie *Freedom Writers*. It inspired me deeply. Brought tears to my eyes. Made me want to be and do and give more. Made me want to improve things. Profoundly.

One of the things I took away from the film is that leadership is all about believing in others (and yourself) when no one else does. The kids in the movie were gang members. Tough lives. Hard hearts. But their teacher saw them for what they truly were: smart/good/caring human beings who'd been knocked down and had given up. The school wouldn't even give them new books—didn't think they were worth it. But their teacher did. Treated them with respect. Bought the books herself (worked two extra jobs to do it). She challenged them. Celebrated them. Believed in them. And they transformed. Because when you see the best in people, they'll give you their best.

I've seen it happen in organizations around the world. Develop, honor and inspire people, and they will fly. As the wonderful teacher Leo Buscaglia once said, "Too often we underestimate the power of a touch, a smile, a kind word, a listening ear, an honest compliment or the smallest act of caring—all of which have the potential to turn a life around."

Leadership is all about believing in others (and yourself) when no one else does.

54

THE BEST PRACTICE IS PRACTICE

Imagine Lance Armstrong stopping his spectacularly disciplined daily practice regimen and still hoping to win the Tour de France. Imagine Steve Nash giving up his crushing daily workouts and post-game analyses and still expecting to be in his finest form. Just think about Tiger relaxing his extraordinary commitment to never-ending refinement and improvement of his golf game. Ridiculous, you say. And yet how many of us, on the playing field of business and life, are devoted to consistent daily practice? Few.

How can you get better if you don't practice? Success doesn't just occur. Brilliant results don't just show up by chance. The finest things in life take patience, focus and sacrifice. To get to world class, you need to work at it. Daily. Relentlessly. Passionately.

Just hoping you'll get to great as a leader (and human being) is nothing more than magical thinking. It's a waste of time. Remember the 1 percent wins. *A few little improvements each day, the result of your daily practice, amount to staggering results over time.* Athletes get better through practicing their sport. Leaders get better by cultivating their craft. By elevating their skills. By deepening their impact. By consciously stepping toward their mountaintops. Until they get there.

Brilliant results don't just show up by chance. The finest things in life take patience, focus and sacrifice.

55

PAIN SERVES YOU WELL

I'm rereading an excellent book called *What Happy People Know*, by Dan Baker, a psychologist and the director of the Life Enhancement Program at Canyon Ranch. I want to share a few of his words with you, on the subject of optimism and dealing with life's trials elegantly and with grace.

When he was younger, his newborn son died. That event devastated him and plunged him into dark despair. In the book he writes of his lessons and says that through his challenges, "I learned what optimism really is: it's knowing that the more painful the event, the more profound the lesson. There are so many lessons in this life we just don't want to learn. You just can't tell someone these things and expect him to become wise. Wisdom only comes the hard way."

Profound words. Perhaps the things that break our hearts are the very things that serve to open them. Pain can serve us so well (if we choose to learn the lessons that it carries). And just maybe life's greatest challenges present its biggest opportunities.

Perhaps the things that break our hearts are the very things that serve to open them.

56

YOUR TEAM'S ONLY AS GOOD AS YOU

Watched a road crew at work this morning while walking Colby to school. The team leader was having a bad day. A bus driver was hitting her horn because a traffic barricade was slowing her down. The team leader yelled, threw a fist into the air and then kicked over the barricade. One angry man.

Then he started yelling at his crew. Mocking them. Spitting out his venom. Ranting like a madman. They looked down at the ground and kept on working. I sense they felt humiliated by the public spectacle. But their leader continued. Pouring his toxic waste out onto the busy street for all to see. Tonight he'll blame his crew for a low-performance day. And probably scream at his kids.

Big idea: Your team will never be greater than you are (even if you are not the team leader). You set the standard to which you all can rise. Each finger affects the strength of the hand. When organizations bring me in to help their people get to world-class performance and create extraordinary results, I gently remind everyone in the room that "everything begins with you." I suggest that's a mission-critical idea. Forget blaming others—that's just excusing yourself. And it all starts with your inner world. External leadership begins with internal mastery. You can't help in the building of an excellent organization until you commit to becoming an excellent person.

That team leader I saw out on the street might want to look in the mirror. Might want to clean up his own messes. Deal with his personal anger. Work on his limiting beliefs. Develop his own character. Open his own heart. "Soft stuff, Robin," you say? No, I really don't think so. It's hard stuff. (How many people have the courage to do it?) The stuff that ultimately drives better business results. Boosts profits. Gets organizations to greatness. And did I mention that it all starts with you? Because it really does.

You set the standard to which you all can rise. Each finger affects the strength of the hand.

57

MUSIC MAKES LIFE BETTER

It's 4 a.m. I'm drinking coffee. The kids are sleeping. And I'm writing in my journal. (Journaling is all about having a conversation with yourself. Helps you build a superior you.) Reflecting. And listening to Maná's CD *Amar Es Combatir*. I love it. Here's the question: How much music do you invite into your life?

Music has helped me get through very painful times. It's offered me inspiration when I needed it, joy when I craved it and peace when I ached for it. It made me a more colorful, engaged and alive human being. I suggest that to live and work at your best, we need to be overflowing with passion, happiness and a relentless desire to win. Music will help. A lot. It will make every moment better. It *is* the soundtrack to a brilliant life. And you can start with Maná.

Music will help. A lot.
It will make every moment better.
It is the soundtrack to a brilliant life.

58

DON'T FIGHT FOR YOUR EXCUSES

"I can't be better than I am at work." "I don't have the time to exercise." "I can't do this project (or reach that dream) because it's too hard/scary/impractical." It's so very human to fight for your excuses. And the more you fight for them, the more they'll own you. Don't feed what you don't want. Let them go. And step into your power.

"We have forty million reasons for failure—but not a single excuse," observed Rudyard Kipling. Successful people don't make excuses. They create results. And no great life was ever built on a foundation of excuses. So stop making them. Most of them are self-created delusions, designed to help you avoid doing the things you are afraid to do. Yes, beneath every excuse lives a fear. A fear of changing. A fear of the unknown. A fear of failure. A fear of success.

Today can be the day you burn the bridges that lead to your excuses (*please* do). Today can be the day you step up to the possibilities that lie just off the beaten path of your life. Today can be the day you Lead Without Title. And access your genuine greatness.

No great life was ever built on a foundation of excuses. So stop making them.

59

ABC (ALWAYS BE CONNECTING)

Leadership has so much to do with relationships. True leaders build strong social networks and trusted communities of teammates, suppliers and customers that will help them get to where they're going (while they, in turn, reciprocate). And exceptional leaders know how to connect. Extremely well.

I'm on the flight home from Hong Kong as I blog on my BlackBerry. A pleasant Air Canada flight attendant has been finding ways to connect with her passengers all through the trip. She remembers our names. And she makes us smile. She just asked if I wanted to eat. I said no (I try to eat little when I fly). Her reply was a classic: "I guess you've had an elegant sufficiency of enoughness." Made me laugh—which made her even more memorable.

So find ways to connect. With the people you work with. With the loved ones you live with. And with the strangers with whom you share this journey called life. You'll not only attract more professional success, you'll also become a happier person.

Find ways to connect. With the people you work with. With the loved ones you live with. And with the strangers with whom you share this journey called life.

60

WHAT SEPARATES YOU?

Starbury One basketball shoes look a lot like those peddled by Nike and Reebok. They are worn on-court by N.Y. Knicks guard Stephon Marbury. And they are built to last, like those of their competitors. So what makes them special? The fact that they are only $14.98 a pair (really). The best businesses know their Separation Points—their competitive advantages—and then have the discipline to stay brilliantly focused on them until the whole world knows what makes them special. Tesla just put out a sports car— $100,000 a pop. But here's the thing: It does 0 to 60 mph in four seconds, is electric powered and will go 100,000 miles per battery. Masterful Separation Points.

So have the courage to be different. Have the boldness within your industry to create value that has never before been created. Be strikingly creative, always getting better and dreaming bigger. And know what separates you from everyone else. Because if you don't know what makes your business special, how can you tell everyone else?

Know what separates you from everyone else. Because if you don't know what makes your business special, how can you tell everyone else?

61

TIME PASSES TOO FAST

Dropped Bianca off at school today. Watched her walking away from me. Toward her friends. She's 11 now. Growing up. Seems like yesterday I carried her around on my back and bought her bubble gum and watched her coloring with crayons. Now she's into Avril Lavigne and Beyoncé and Hilary Duff. As I mentioned earlier, she wants to be a rock drummer when she grows up. (When she was younger, she wanted to be a dentist—and a dollar-store owner.)

One of my favorite music artists (musicians really are artists), English songwriter Lloyd Cole, has a song that reminds us that time is a lot like an airplane, flying by too fast. Don't blink. Before you know it, your kids will be gone, off living lives of their own. Time's like that. Slips through our fingers like grains of sand. So today, please do love your loved ones. Give your best at work. Go the extra mile in all you do. Speak truthfully. Live with honor. And have some fun. Because one day, your time will run out.

Go the extra mile in all you do.
Speak truthfully. Live with honor.
And have some fun. Because one day,
your time will run out.

62

WHAT HAPPENED TO QUIET?

I was in an airport, about to fly to Las Vegas and give a speech to 3,000 network marketers. Had some time, so went up to the business lounge to read. Too noisy. Cell phones rang (with those grating ring tones that cause me to toss in my sleep). People talked too loud on their BlackBerries (RIM is one of our clients—still love you guys). One passenger was playing an electronic game on a PlayStation Portable, sans earpiece. So we all heard him as he battled the dragons and invaded new lands (kind of funny, actually). I shut out the world courtesy of my iPod. Thanks, Steve Jobs. But I shouldn't have had to.

Then I went to the gate. Guess what? Noise. Noise. Noise. Someone had installed three flat-screen TVs there—the volume now at 10. Pretty hard to believe. Not everyone was in the mood to watch TV, or wanted the interruption. No one asked for our permission. Again, out came the iPod. I need my peace. Crave it, actually. (I believe world-class results come from alternating periods of peak performance with periods of deep renewal; big idea there.)

Sure, I appreciate technology. Helps us work better and live better, if used intelligently. But whatever happened to silent spaces and noiseless places? Too much noise gets in the way of dreaming and good conversations and time to just be. And we all need that. If we want to live a good life. And get to great.

Too much noise gets in the way of dreaming and good conversations and time to just be.

63

A STAINLESS CHARACTER

Stainless steel—a tremendous invention. But what about a stainless character? One that is noble, aspires for mastery in all pursuits and never gives up in moving closer to its ideals. What is within must always appear without. What I mean by that is that the quality of your inner world eventually is reflected in the quality of your outer world. Your external life can never grow bigger than your internal one. Life really is a mirror— reflecting who we are, rather than all we want.

A person who dreams pristine dreams and who is impeccably honest, good, ethical and stands for what's best will soon act in alignment with those values. And those actions cannot help but drive extraordinary results. Inner always creates outer. Always.

Last night I saw *Spiderman 3* with Bianca. Best line in the movie was the most obvious one: "We always have a choice. We can always choose between right and wrong." This leadership/success/greatness stuff really is pretty simple. Simple—but not easy (and excellence is all about doing what's right versus what's easy). The best things in life do take effort and commitment and discipline. (My friend Nido Qubein once said, "The price of discipline is always less than the pain of regret.") And sure, it all seems so obvious. But what's most obvious is what's most often forgotten.

"We always have a choice. We can always choose between right and wrong."

64

SET PEOPLE FREE

The best leaders turn their teammates loose. They clearly communicate the vision, coach and develop their people and, once done, set them free. Free to use their own creativity and ingenuity to get the results needed. Free to do excellent work and find splendid solutions. Free to feel what it's like to succeed. And free to fail, because making mistakes is part of getting to success.

People want to be a part of an organization that lets them bring their gifts to work and be fully alive. People want to be engaged and feel proud of their contribution. At the deepest level, each of us aches to know the work we do—and the lives we lead—make a difference. Will you let the people around you realize this longing by setting them free? Because if you don't, someone else will.

People want to be a part of an organization that lets them bring their gifts to work and be fully alive.

65

A DAY OF LISTENING

Listening is, in so many ways, the social equity of the world-class cultures that evolve into world-class organizations. Listening makes people feel special (and talent leaves organizations mainly because they didn't feel special). Listening shows respect. Listening allows you to gather the data that will improve everything you do. I guess what I'm suggesting to you is that brilliant performers are brilliant listeners.

Today, just for a day, make the decision to listen (versus just hear). Don't interrupt. Don't rehearse your answer while the other person is speaking. And don't dare check your e-mail or search for text messages while another human being is sharing their words. Just listen. Deeply. Be there for that person. Because everyone has a voice. And each of us craves to have ours recognized. Watch the great things that unfold once you do.

Everyone has a voice. And each of us craves to have ours recognized.

66

SMART COMPANIES COMPETE FOR EMOTION

Powerful thought: The main competition is not for "share of wallet" (as I hear at so many of my clients' conferences). No. It's for share of your customers' hearts. In today's world of business, what smart companies compete for are the emotions of the people they serve.

People buy with their emotions. I drink Colombian coffee. Why? Because it tastes extraordinary, and makes me feel happy. I try to buy from companies with a social conscience. Why? Because doing so makes me feel good about myself. I adore my old, ripped Levi's. Why? Because they make me feel relaxed—and grounded. That's all emotional engagement.

I love staying at the Mercer in New York and Hotel Victor in Miami and the Savoy in Florence and the Ritz-Carlton in Singapore and the Leela Palace Hotel in Goa. Why? Because they wow me. And make me feel special (there's that feeling thing again).

Connect with your customers' heads and your product or service may be seen as a commodity: They'll leave you when a competitor comes in at a cheaper price. But connect with their hearts and you can have them for a lifetime. Great businesses don't have customers who like them. They have customers who *love* them. And that's what allows them to endure.

The main competition is not for "share of wallet." No. It's for share of your customers' hearts.

67

YOU'LL KNOW WHEN YOU KNOW

I did a show on SIRIUS Satellite Radio yesterday. The host, Jesse Dylan, asked me a thoughtful question: "Robin, we all have goals and aspirations. But sometimes things don't go as planned. How do you know when to quit?" My answer was straightforward: "You'll know when you know."

No one gets to world class in their work or within their personal lives without a relentless devotion to not giving up. All acts of heroism were accomplished by human beings who refused to lose. They just wouldn't let go—no matter how bad or impossible or impractical things looked. But having said that, life often sends us curve balls and has other plans for us. (Comedian Gilda Radner, who died of ovarian cancer at age 42, put it so very well: "Now I've learned the hard way that some poems don't rhyme and some stories don't have a clear beginning, middle and end. Life is about not knowing, having to change, taking the moment and making the most of it without knowing what's going to happen next. Delicious ambiguity.")

We long for something to happen and some dream to get done. But no matter how hard we try, the clouds never part. We never get the break. Luck never smiles on us. We continue to toil in darkness, fueled purely by faith. That's fine—if deep within you your fire burns brightly and every fiber within you tells you to carry on (self-faith is a hallmark of greatness). But sometimes, you get to a point where you just know it's time to change strategy. It's not about losing hope. You just *know*. It's about trusting life. Trusting that there's an even better thing waiting for you. And that it's time to course-correct.

For the past few years, I've tried to live by the pretty simple philosophy that I shared with you in an earlier chapter: Do your best and let life do the rest. It's not easy to let go of what you want (I know how painful that can be). But why wouldn't you, if something even better is waiting just around the corner?

Do your best and let life do the rest.

68

BE A HERO

On a recent flight with Colby, I flipped through the newspapers while he read a Hardy Boys book. Saw an article about Tristan Unsworth, an 11-year-old boy who is now the hero of his small hometown in Canada. The other day, his snowboarding buddy was sitting next to him in class, sucking on a candy. Someone said something funny, the kids started to laugh, and that sent the candy down the boy's windpipe. Everyone in the classroom was too stunned to do much. The boy started choking. His face turned purple. He said later that he thought it was his day to die. But Tristan's grandmother had taught him the Heimlich maneuver. He rushed into action, and saved his friend's life. Beautiful.

The school principal said yesterday, "He's the most humble boy I've ever met in my entire life. He's the most wonderful boy." A powerful reminder for you: Greatness inhabits each one of us. And that's true whether you are an entrepreneur in Moscow or a teacher in Tel Aviv or a student in Bogotá or a manager in Manila. Let's not forget that. Let's not mask our brilliance. Let's not bury it so deep that we neglect the essence of who we are. Let's model ourselves after Tristan. And be remarkable.

Greatness inhabits each one of us.
And that's true whether you are an
entrepreneur in Moscow or a teacher
in Tel Aviv or a student in Bogotá or
a manager in Manila.

69

WHY PLAN?

Personal planning and goal-setting are not sexy topics. But they are incredibly important and central to an extraordinary experience of life. I see it time and time again among the clients who I coach: lots of time spent articulating a clear and detailed vision for what the key areas of their lives will look like, then a written plan with the vision broken down into sequenced goals so that the vision isn't so overwhelming and the big picture can be seen as manageable steps to drive daily action.

One of the best effects of planning that I've discovered personally is what it does to my mind. Let me put it this way: Few things focus the mind as well as setting plans on paper and then sequencing them into goals. The very act of doing it heightens your awareness as to what's most important. And with better awareness, you will make better choices. And as you make better choices, you are certain to experience better results.

So give yourself a gift: Take out a nice, crisp white sheet of paper. Sharpen a pencil. And then start writing about the work and home you desire to create. It's a lot easier than you may think. And the results will stun you.

Give yourself a gift:
Take out a nice, crisp white sheet
of paper. Sharpen a pencil. And then
start writing about the work and
home you desire to create.

70

ASK TO GET

You'll never know if you don't even try. There is enormous power in asking for what you want. All too often, our internal chatter prevents us from taking the steps needed to get us to our own unique form of greatness. We are kept small from our inner imaginings—so many of which are lies.

The most brilliant of the best, those who live glorious lives that matter, ask like crazy. They understand that it's a habit that must be polished for it to shine. And the more you do it, the easier it gets (like any skill). So they ask. For the support and help they need at work. For the understanding they may seek at home. For a win they need for their business. For a better table at their favorite restaurant. For a better seat at a sold-out concert. And because they ask more, they get more (success always has been a numbers game).

Nothing happens until you ask. People are not mind readers. They need to know what's meaningful to you. And if you ask nicely, they just might say yes.

The most brilliant of the best,
those who live glorious lives that
matter, ask like crazy.

71

DO NEW THINGS

Human beings crave control—that's just the way we are. It's a survival mechanism that goes right back to the days when we lived in caves. We need certainty, and anything less makes us uncomfortable. But leadership is all about getting good at being *uncomfortable*. It's about running toward, not away from, the things that intimidate and frighten you. And leadership is about trying new things.

It's so easy to eat the same food each day. But if you don't try new foods, you just might miss out on the opportunity to discover your new favorite meal. It's easy to associate with the same people and have the same conversations each day. But if you don't expand your community, you just might miss out on meeting your new best friend. It's so easy to do the same things at work each day—to get stuck in a rut. And if you don't stretch, you'll miss an achievement that could flood you with a sense of confidence and fulfillment that will be the start of a whole new world of work.

So I invite you to use each day as a platform for filling your life with more adventure, passion and energy by injecting into it more new things. Listen to Boozoo Bajou if you usually listen to

Bach. Eat Malaysian food if you usually do meat and potatoes. Read *Dwell* magazine if you subscribe to *Fortune*. It's a big, interesting world out there. And it's yours for the taking.

Listen to Boozoo Bajou if you usually listen to Bach. Eat Malaysian food if you usually do meat and potatoes. Read Dwell *magazine if you subscribe to* Fortune.

72

ON PERSONAL MASTERY

Two beautiful words: *personal mastery*. They have an inspirational vibe to them. They offer hope. They challenge. They provoke. They affirm—and remind us of our highest possibilities.

To be given the gift of life is to be given an awesome responsibility. Each of us must go out into the world each day and live our best. Yes, life doesn't always seem fair. We'll encounter difficult customers and low-performing suppliers and angry commuters. We'll face hard and confusing times. We'll feel alone, or like giving up on standing for our highest and best. That's just life happening. But, at the same time, life offers you daily opportunities to shine. To polish your gifts. To release your chains. To achieve personal mastery.

Make a commitment today that will alter the course of your life. Forever. Dedicate yourself to personal *mastery*. Think about your thinking. Detect your authentic values and what you aim to stand for. (How can you be who you are if you don't know who you are?) Get to know your fears. Reflect on your personal genius and human potential. Learn to let go of the emotional baggage from you past. Refuse to tolerate negativity. (Kahlil Gibran once wrote that "Doubt is a pain too lonely to know that faith is his twin brother"; every one of us has so many more choices than we can currently see, and as we dare, doors we didn't even know existed begin to open up.) Read more. Learn more. Get fit—no, get *ultra* fit (sad that—too often— good health only matters to those who have lost it). Become remarkable at what you do for work. Become so good at your craft that your organization cannot run without you. Become the friendliest person you know. Work on compassion and understanding. Be nice. Be good.

Life offers you daily opportunities to shine. To polish your gifts. To release your chains. To achieve personal mastery.

73

BE UNPOPULAR

If you read my blog regularly, you know I'm a fan of Ian Schrager's hotels. Stayed in my first one nearly a decade ago when I did the U.S. book tour for *The Monk Who Sold His Ferrari* (the Paramount in NYC). In *The Greatness Guide* I wrote about St Martins Lane in London (still one of my all-time favorite hotels on the planet). Why do I like Schrager's hotels? Because, when they first came out, they were unlike anything else (now most boutique hotels have some of the elements from the early Schrager days). They are unforgettably cool. They have the confidence to be part modern art gallery and part place to sleep. They lead rather than follow—like all the best businesses (and human beings).

I'm reading a splendid book by Harry Beckwith called *What Clients Love* this morning as I drink my Colombian coffee. Reflecting on business and on life. In the book, Beckwith quotes Schrager who, true to form, says, "Let twenty-four despise [my hotels] for all I care— just so one in twenty-five love them." The big idea for us: Businesses that try to be all things to all people end up being nothing to anyone. You need to stand for something. You need to play ferociously. Passionately. Emotionally. To get to world class. Or don't play at all.

The big idea for us:
Businesses that try to be all
things to all people end up being
nothing to anyone.

74

OWN YOUR GREATNESS

Read a letter scribbled in pencil from an inmate in an American prison this a.m. He said *The Monk Who Sold His Ferrari* changed his life. Because it helped him remember that he was made to make a difference and realize his potential. He'd forgotten who he was meant to be. Because life had hurt him. A lot.

I hear this all the time. People appreciate being reminded that they are meant to play at great. That there are no extra people on the planet. That every life has a purpose. We knew these truths as kids. So we dreamed. We reached. We acted fearlessly. Lived life passionately. And stood in possibility. But we lost that wisdom—as we grew up and walked farther out into the world, away from our Real Nature.

Maybe self-improvement is a waste of time. Maybe *self-remembering* (and reconnecting to the brilliance/creativity/authenticity/greatness you once knew) is where the action is. Lots of letters to me from *The Greatness Guide* readers speak of this. That life has a habit of making us forget. We fall into routine. We take things for granted. We stop taking risks. We stop aiming for the mountaintop. We stop speaking truth. We play small with the gift of our lives. But we deserve better than mediocrity. Ordinary people can do remarkable things. By recalling who they truly are. And living at their best.

People appreciate being reminded
that they are meant to play at great. That
there are no extra people on the planet.
That every life has a purpose.

75

BE LIKE COLDPLAY

I saw Coldplay in Toronto a while ago. For two hours they rocked the stadium with nearly 20,000 people on their feet, cheering. I had an amazing time, and finally realized why the pundits are saying "Coldplay is the next U2." I also got a bunch of leadership ideas from watching the band that I hope you will use to get to your next level.

The four Big Ideas. First, from start to finish, they understood what they were there for: to create an experience for their clients. The lighting was superb, the visuals were world class, and the staging was perfect. Second, they engaged the audience and made us part of the show. They had us singing, dancing and laughing. Third, they showed us love. (How many businesses actually show you love and make you feel special when you do business with them? Well, Coldplay did.) They thanked us for making them so successful, they showed genuine gratitude and they seemed truly humble (and people connect with vulnerability). And fourth, they were really good at what they did. Fantastic songs with great delivery.

Yes, Coldplay over-delivered. And guess what—because of that, I'm a real fan. My challenge to you: Be the Coldplay of your market space. Create fans, then delight them. And do whatever it takes to get them coming back for more.

Create fans, then delight them. And do whatever it takes to get them coming back for more.

76

STOP SLEEPING SO MUCH

I know I'm unpopular on this point but I owe you my truth: Most people sleep more than they need to. They fall into the trap of spending some of the best hours of their lives on a mattress. They squander their potentially breathtaking gifts. They lose the battle of the bed. They trade their greatness for a snooze button.

Here's an insight I invite you to consider: Sleep begets sleep. The more sleep you take, the more you need. Ever noticed that as you sleep more, you feel sleepier? Strange, isn't it. But it's true.

Yes, I get that sleep is essential to keep us radiant, renewed and healthy. My fear is *too much* sleep. The kind that keeps great people ordinary. The kind that minimizes high-potential lives. The kind that sucks the living out of human beings destined to stand for excellence (and you know who you are). Happens to a lot of us. Because we fall in love with a pillow.

Too many important things to do and too many great places to explore and too many Big Hairy Audacious Goals (thanks, Jim Collins) to get, for us to sleep too much. Life is for the living. I need to repeat that: Life is for the Living. You and I have been given a gift today: to have the opportunity to make a difference and exercise our talents and have a phenomenally fun time doing it. And we need to seize (and respect) that gift. So sleep less. Live more. And as Benjamin Franklin observed, "There will be plenty of time to sleep when you're dead." I've always liked that guy.

My fear is too much sleep. The kind that keeps great people ordinary. The kind that minimizes high-potential lives.

77

GO PERPENDICULAR

In Italy on vacation with the kids. Working on a new book too. The writing's going really well. And I'm doing some relaxing and renewing. I've never eaten so much pasta in my life. I'm keeping our neighborhood trattoria in business. (Maybe my next project should be a diet book?)

Yesterday afternoon the kids and I rented a little boat and headed down the Amalfi Coast. We hugged the shoreline, stayed close to land, never strayed far from home. This got me thinking. About Christopher Columbus. And about taking smart risks.

Every explorer before him feared losing sight of the shore. They clung to the known. They opted for security. They didn't dare. Columbus did something different. He was brave. Went straight out to sea. Went perpendicular to the shoreline. And found a new world. Good on him.

Of course I needed to be safe with my kids. I'm just trying to make a point: Greatness, as a leader and as a human, sometimes requires that you leave the constraints of safety. Sometimes you just have to let go of the known. And sail out into the unknown. To try a new way. To think a new thought. To behave in a new way. And to go perpendicular when the rest of the world hugs the shoreline and clings to safety. Yes—I get it's *so* human to feel frightened as we experiennce the Blue Ocean of Change, transition and growth. But as Lord Chesterfield said, "It is not possible to discover new oceans unless one is willing to lose sight of the shore."

"It is not possible to discover new oceans unless one is willing to lose sight of the shore."

78

DO YOUR LIFE

It's a serene Sunday morning as I write this chapter. "Café del Mar" plays while I enjoy a delicious cup of java. My kids are reading and I'm moving in slow motion. Love it.

Something happened a little earlier that made me laugh, and I want to share it with you. Bianca and I were playing. Role-playing to be precise. She was pretending to be me and I was being her. She sat in my study and wrote in my journal, mimicking the way I speak. I, in turn, talked nonstop about dogs, rock bands and hip CDs. After a few minutes of imitating me, here's what she said (honestly): "I don't want to be you anymore, Dad. It's too hard. I just want to be me." Perfect.

What's more important in life than being yourself (and loving who you are)? Most of us really do end up living someone else's life. And we dismiss happiness as a result. Fulfillment comes from living your truth. Doing your values. Pursuing your desires and ideals. "To thine own self be true," wrote that British sage, Shakespeare. No point in getting to the end and realizing you never let the real you come out to play. An excellent life grows out of an authentic one. Truly.

An excellent life grows out of
an authentic one.

79

GIVE TO GET

Walking down the street today I heard a man repeating this mantra to all those who passed by him: "Have you helped someone today besides yourself?" He was trying to raise money. For his Cause. But it got me thinking about giving. You need to give to get. Giving does begin the receiving process.

Give support to get it. Give praise to receive it. Give your best to attract it. Give more respect to experience it. And give more love to become beloved. (Powerful thought: If you make five people feel better about themselves each day, by the end of one year you will singlehandedly have elevated the lives of nearly 2,000 people. Continue this practice and—after a decade—you'll have positively impacted 20,000 people. Factor in the number of people that those you touch, in turn, influence and you'll quickly realize that your "little daily gestures of inspiration" can end up helping hundreds of thousands of human beings over the course of your lifetime.)

Give to get. Nice refrain. And so staggeringly simple (as the truest ideas are). All about servant leadership. Help others reach world class. And they'll joyfully help you get to your cherished ideals.

*You need to give to get. Giving does begin
the receiving process.*

80

BE LIKE J.K.

The very nature of a visionary is that they see what others miss. (Makes me think of what the German philosopher Arthur Schopenhauer once said: "Talent hits a target no one else can hit; genius hits a target no one else can see.") It's like an inside joke that only they get: They see this vivid dream/opportunity/desire in their imaginations and then spend their days breathing life into it—even though everyone around them thinks they're wasting their time, or are eccentric, or foolhardy or even crazy. Think Gandhi. Think Edison. Think Disney. Think J.K.

J.K. Rowling was a single mother struggling to pay her bills when the idea of a book about a misfit young wizard downloaded into her mind over a four-hour train ride. She says on her website that she feels blessed she had no pen with her at the time, because writing down all the miraculous ideas that were coming to her would have slowed the flow. Once the manuscript was done, her agent began to send Harry Potter to publishers. Most rejected the book instantly. One didn't. And that's my point about visionaries: They see an opportunity that most around them just don't get. Imagine that. Rejecting Harry Potter. Thinking no one would buy the book. Missing out on one of the best-selling books in the history of humankind.

Being a visionary and stepping into the higher reaches of your life necessarily means dealing with the fact that people will question you. They will not get where you are going. They might call you odd or foolish or unorthodox. They will laugh at you. All good. Thank them for the compliments and keep doing what you need to do to get to where you need to get. The world will be a better place once you do. As Maya Angelou observed, "If one is lucky, a solitary fantasy can transform a million realities."

And that's my point about visionaries: They see an opportunity that most around them just don't get. Imagine that. Rejecting Harry Potter.

81

WHATEVER HAPPENED TO COMMITMENT?

When I was in Dubai delivering a leadership presentation for the Young Presidents' Organization a while ago, a woman approached me and said, "Robin, I loved reading *The Monk Who Sold His Ferrari*, but you make it all sound so easy. Making improvements in my life is hard." Hmm. Made me think. A lot. Here's where I'm at with that one.

We live in a world seduced by the easy. We want to look great and be spectacularly fit but we don't want to have to exercise to get there. We want to be successful in our careers but we wonder if there's a way to reach world class without having to work hard and be disciplined (every great executive is strikingly disciplined, as is every great company). We dream of living fearless, joy-filled lives, but we all too often avoid the very best practices (like getting up early, taking risks, setting goals and reading) that are certain to deliver us to our ideals. Nothing comes for free. There truly are no free lunches. The best things in life require sacrifice and devotion. Each of us, to get to our own unique forms of personal and professional greatness, must pay the price. And the more we pay, the more we'll receive.

Wanting to live your best life, at work and at home, without having to work at it and stay disciplined around our important To

Do's, is like wanting an amazing garden without having to plant anything. Or like hoping to be in superb physical condition without having to give up the daily chocolate bar. Or like praying to have a great business by swallowing some magic pill. Whatever happened to commitment? And dedication?

Great lives don't just occur out of the blue. They are crafted and built, like the Taj Mahal and the Great Wall of China, block by block, day by day. And superb businesses don't just appear. They are forged through continuous and never-ending improvement and effort. Let's not fall into believing that the best things in life come without effort. Give your best, and the best will come to you. Guaranteed.

Nothing comes for free. There truly are no free lunches. The best things in life require sacrifice and devotion.

82

GET EXCITED OR GET UPSET

The most important of all of our human traits is the power we have to choose. To choose how we live. To choose what we will do. To choose how we will view and consider a circumstance.

I'm up here in the mountains on a quick ski trip with my kids. Yesterday it rained. We could have grumbled. We could have complained. We could have got frustrated. Instead, we stepped back, decided to make a better choice and then viewed the whole thing as a giant adventure. We got excited versus upset. We donned the plastic covers that the resort provided. Suited up. And skied like there was no tomorrow. Guess what? The skiing was actually amazing. Soft snow. No crowds. Clean runs. It's going to take me a week to wipe the smile off my face. Each day we have the opportunity to make choices. And the way we choose shapes our destiny. So don't get upset. Get excited. As author Paul Theroux once observed, "Only a fool blames his bad vacation on the rain."

Each day we have the opportunity to make choices. And the way we choose shapes our destiny.

83

BUILD BRIDGES, NOT FENCES

Had a conversation with a VIP today (Very Interesting Person). Thirty-two years old. Grew up in the Caribbean. Builds fences for a living. A philosopher at heart.

Told me how everyone is into building fences these days. To block out their neighbors. To insulate themselves. To maintain privacy. And to foster separateness. "I grew up in St. Vincent," he shared. "On our little island, we were like one big family. It really took a village to raise each child. Everyone talked to each other. People cared about one another. We were part of each other's lives—a real community."

Community. Beautiful word. Every single one of us has a deep psychological need for it. We all crave to belong. To know we are part of a larger whole. It gives us a sense of security. Safety. And happiness. The best organizations foster community and build workplaces where people feel safe to be themselves again. The best families do the same thing—honoring each other and creating rich shared moments. So maybe we should stop worrying so much about building fences. And start creating true security—by building bridges.

We all crave to belong.
To know we are part of a larger whole.

84

FAIL FASTER

Full disclosure: I'm not the first to use the term "fail faster." But I do love it. The CEO of Coca-Cola at the annual meeting informed shareholders that the company was now going on an innovation tear and that his organization's reinvention plan was contained in a document entitled "The Manifesto for Growth." He noted that spending on marketing and innovation would increase by US$400 million and then—and here's the big line—observed, "You will see some failures. As we take more risks, this is something we must accept as part of the regeneration process." Which brings me to the imperative of Failing Fast.

At a leadership presentation I gave a while ago to the sales team of a large pharmaceutical company, someone came up to me afterwards and said, "Robin, I loved your speech. Especially the idea about failure being the price of greatness." That reminded me that too many of us are so afraid of failure that we don't even try (Seneca once said, "It is not because things are difficult that we do not dare. It is because we do not dare that things are difficult"). Many of us are frightened of looking silly or being embarrassed by failure and as a result, we don't take the risk and seize an opportunity. We think failure is bad. It isn't. It's good. No, it's great.

There can be no success without failure. It's just part of the process. The companies and people who have reached the heights of success are the same ones that have failed the most often. You need to fail to win. And the faster you fail, the more quickly you'll learn precisely what you need to do to win. So Fail Fast. Out-fail the competition. Out-fail the person you once were. I'll leave you with a quote from Robert F. Kennedy: "Only those who dare to fail greatly can ever achieve greatly."

There can be no success without failure.
It's just part of the process. . . .
You need to fail to win.

85

ANGELS IN YOUR EVOLUTION

An idea just came to me. You've heard it before, but the more we get exposed to a good idea, the more deeply we get to integrate it. Like reading a powerful book for a second and third time. Seems like a whole new book on every new reading. Did the book change? No. You did. Your capacity to understand got bigger. Your world-view got broader. Your ability to take in the insights grew. And so you discovered a whole new level of knowledge in that book. That was always there. You just didn't have the eyes to see it before.

The idea I feel so passionately about on this sunny afternoon can be stated in a simple phrase: Angels of Evolution. Nothing soft and irrelevant about this one. Just a way to look at life's challenges in a better light. As blessings rather than curses. Because they just might be. Angels of Evolution. Everyone who is causing you stress, struggle and challenge in your life just might be an angel of sorts. They just might be the very messengers carrying the lessons you most need to learn to get to your Next Level of Greatness.

The difficult teammate might be an angel of sorts, here to teach you understanding. The mean salesclerk might be an angel showing up to help you with compassion or communication or standing up for yourself. A business setback or professional disappointment might be an angel sent to build your resolve and commitment. A health issue might be an angelic wakeup call to get you to commit to a better diet, regular exercise, relaxation and meditation. Each encounter represents a defining moment that gets you to the excellence meant for you.

Angels of Evolution. The hardest stuff in your life is the ideal stuff to get you to where you've always dreamed of being. The people and events that irritate, anger and hurt you are the ideal educators to help you learn the lessons that will help you shine— at work, at home and in life. So that you evolve. And grow.

Everyone who is causing you stress, struggle and challenge in your life just might be an angel of sorts . . . carrying the lessons you most need to learn.

86

LEAD BY EXAMPLE

I had a conversation with an old friend the other day. He's done some tremendous things with his business and carved out a meaningful life. He said something that I wanted to share with you. Because it speaks to the best way to influence other people. Leadership by example.

"Robin," he said, "the greatest sermon in life is the one you see." To me that meant, Make your life your message. Live your truth. Walk your values. Behave your philosophy. That's how you move those around you to play at their best.

It's so easy to talk a great game. Far harder to live it. But the great ones do. Elegantly. Consistently. Passionately. As famed psychologist Abraham Maslow said, "In order for us to become truly happy, that which we can become, we must become."

*"The greatest sermon in life
is the one you see."*

87

BE AN IDEA FACTORY

One big idea could revolutionize your life—and even the world around you. All it takes is that single genius thought to change the whole game. I'm reading a fantastic book called *Humble Masterpieces: Everyday Marvels of Design* by Paola Antonelli, curator of architecture and design at New York's Museum of Modern Art. In one of the (little) chapters, I learned of designer Daniel Cudzik. He's the brave dreamer who invented the stay-on metal tab that you now see on every single one of the billion aluminum cans made every year. Before his invention, tabs were pulled off and thrown away, creating tons of litter, not to mention hurt feet. One idea transformed all that.

Cudzik was watching TV one night with his two kids when the vision came to him. (Your best ideas will come when you least expect it. Most revolutionary thoughts don't come when you are keeping a frenetic pace, they come when you're having fun, so have some fun—it's good for business, as well as for your soul.) Rather than letting the idea slip away (like most of us do), he wrote it down, sketching his plan for the stay-on tab. He quickly gave it to a draftsman, and they soon created the prototype. Guess what? It worked. Brings me to my suggestion: Become an idea factory. Of course, you also need to have a passionate commitment to breathing life into your big ideas through near-flawless execution. Couple the two and you just might produce something extraordinarily valuable. And wouldn't that be a wonderful thing?

One big idea could revolutionize your life— and even the world around you. All it takes is that single genius thought to change the whole game.

88

SPEAK YOUR TRUTH

This past weekend the kids and I returned to Halifax, Nova Scotia, an amazing city on the Atlantic Ocean with very special human beings and outrageously good fish and chips (which also happens to be the place where I grew up). We were there to celebrate a friend's fortieth wedding anniversary. As we walked out of a bookstore, a car drove by with a bumper sticker that I'll never forget. It said, SPEAK YOUR TRUTH—EVEN WHEN YOUR VOICE SHAKES. Brilliant.

Too many people talk the good talk these days. Tons of empty promises. And hype. And lofty statements that never amount to anything. True leaders are different. They talk less and do more. I love the quiet leaders. Those silent souls who under-promise and over-deliver. And when they do speak, they speak Truth. The Merchants of Wow among us understand that a person's word is their bond. And that every promise kept builds credibility, the foundation of trust. So make the commitment to be impeccable with your word.

You really can be a leader, no matter what your title is. In the theater they say, "No role is a small role." And in life, no person is an insignificant one. ("Every calling is great when greatly pursued," observed Oliver Wendell Holmes.) Each day, at work and at home, you have an opportunity to create an impact, to make a difference and to reveal your potential. And one of the things that separates leaders from followers is that those who lead speak openly, honestly and courageously. Even when the very thought of doing so frightens them. Even when their voices shake.

One of the things that separates leaders from followers is that those who lead speak openly, honestly and courageously.

89

LEADERSHIP BEGINS AT HOME

I was on my way to a meeting and saw a billboard that caught my eye. Its words: What are you teaching your children? The big idea? Leadership really does begin at home.

What are we teaching our children by the lives we are leading and the examples we are setting? I believe that the best way to influence your kids is to be true to yourself and to lead the best life that you can, so that they will adopt the same values, though their path may be different. What message are you sending to those little leaders who watch your every move and model your every act? Are you showing them what's possible by being remarkable in each of your pursuits? Or are you teaching them to play small by resigning yourself to average?

The fruit never falls far from the tree, and your children will become a lot more like you than you may believe. You can help your kids get to their greatness. It starts with you leading the way.

The fruit never falls far from the tree, and your children will become a lot more like you than you may believe.

90

RESPECT RULES

Eyes sometimes glaze over on the topic of respect in the workplace. The concept is so obvious that it seems not even worth discussing. We all know that if you treat your people well, they'll treat your customers well. We all know that employees excel when they feel cared for, trusted and valued. We all get that everyone wants to work within an organization where they can grow, have friends and be themselves. Or do we?

I just read about a study of 370,378 employees performed by Sirota Survey Intelligence on this seemingly obvious subject of respect at work. Guess what? Out of all those human beings polled, only 21 percent of those in non-management posts felt the respect management gave them was at a "very good" level. Maybe the importance of respect within our organizations isn't as ingrained as we all believe it to be. Splendid opportunity here.

The study confirmed too that the people who felt most respected were also the ones who felt the most loyalty to the companies they worked for. And in a world where attracting—and keeping—superb talent is one of the most critical of all success factors, anything that breeds greater loyalty needs to be done.

So, Respect Rules. Treating people well rocks. Making your team-mates feel special is job number one. Because they are special.

Here are a few practical strategies to unleash respect at work:

- *Say "please" and "thank you."*
- *Be on time (punctuality is a mark of the great ones).*
- *Reward people for excellent performance.*
- *Become a brilliant listener (people will love you for it).*
- *Coach the people you work with and help them realize their potential (we all want to get better).*
- *Write thank-you notes.*
- *Promote candor and truth-telling.*
- *Give people permission to take sensible risks and the freedom to fail.*
- *Encourage creativity and authenticity.*

When people feel respected, they feel better about themselves. And people who feel good, do good.

---

*Making your teammates feel special
is job number one.*

91

LEARN FROM MICHAEL J. FOX

I saw television star Michael J. Fox being interviewed on NBC the other night. You probably know he has Parkinson's disease. The condition would knock most of us down. Not M.J.F. He said that he actually felt Parkinson's brought many blessings into his life, and shared during the interview how it pushed out all the superficial things, making way for much richer ones such as wisdom, understanding and love.

Powerful thought: Life's most painful experiences are the very circumstances that introduce us to our best. During times of ease, we can get caught up in shallow pursuits and pleasures. Hard times cause us to go deep. The unmeaningful stuff falls aside and we awake to what's important. Things like family, friends, relationships, presenting our best to the world, enjoying each day's gifts and leaving the world better than we found it.

Every life is terminal. No matter how long we get to live, we are all headed for the same end. When you remember that before we know it we'll all be dust, the things that currently limit you (like fear, pride and past disappointments) just fall away. And you discover that the time to shine—and be great—really is now.

So thank you, Michael J. Fox. For showing courage and leadership. For speaking honestly. For being a light in a world with far too much darkness.

Every life is terminal.
No matter how long we get to live,
we are all headed for the same end.

92

THE JOURNEY'S AS GOOD AS THE END

Just read something in a Cadillac ad in an issue of *GQ*. It quotes actor Andy Garcia as saying, "It's important, when going after a goal, to never lose sight of the integrity of the journey." I so appreciate the way he languaged that. And he's right. The journey toward any result—whether that result is being amazingly good at what you do for a living or great in the way you conduct your life—is just as important (if not more important) than the end. I guess what I'm inviting you to consider is that the climb offers you far more value and as many rewards as getting to your mountain-top. Why? Because the climb to your ideals shapes your character, offers you opportunities to realize your potential and tests you to see how much you really want to win. It's the climb that teaches you, transforms you and evokes the genius that inhabits you. You get to develop the Qualities of Greatness, such as perseverance/courage/resilience/compassion/understanding. Sure, getting to the dream feels deliciously wonderful. I'll be first to agree with you on that. But it doesn't bring you the same sustained gifts that the journey does. We learn more from the times that test us than we do from times of success.

So the next time you feel impatient or frustrated or hope-less en route to the professional and personal life that you want, remember that precisely where you are might just be the best place you could possibly be. And maybe the journey is better than the destination.

I guess what I'm inviting you to consider is that the climb offers you far more value and as many rewards as getting to your mountaintop.

93

WHAT IS SUCCESS?

To me, success is all about being *in the process* of joyfully creating a life that reflects your highest values, your deepest beliefs and your greatest dreams. There's a lot in that statement and I invite you to break it down and reflect on it. There's the part about the "process" of creating life on your terms (the journey really is better than the end). There's the part about "joyfully" journeying through life because life is meant to be fun. There's the element of living by your values and beliefs, which is all about being true to yourself and living life on your terms. And there's that aspect of chasing your dreams, as these are what get us out of bed each day and fill our hearts with hope.

This reminds me of the words of Mark Twain: "Twenty years from now you will be more disappointed by the things you didn't do than by the ones you did. So throw off the bowlines. Sail away from the safe harbor. Catch the trade winds in your sails. Explore. Dream. Discover." That's true success.

To me, success is all about being in the process of joyfully creating a life that reflects your highest values, your deepest beliefs and your greatest dreams.

94

YOUR HIGHEST FREEDOM

One of my favorite books is *Man's Search for Meaning*, written by Viktor Frankl, an Austrian psychotherapist who survived confinement in Nazi concentration camps. So many of those around him perished. They lost hope. They fell into despair, then death. He managed to get through the ordeal by applying what I believe is our highest human freedom: our ability to choose how we respond to and process any event that happens to us. We can look for some good or we can become haunted by the bad. Frankl writes, "Everything can be taken from a man but one thing, the last of the human freedoms to choose one's attitude to a given set of circumstances, to choose one's way." Such a magnificent thought.

"Everything can be taken from a man but one thing, the last of the human freedoms to choose one's attitude to a given set of circumstances, to choose one's way."

95

GO HOLLYWOOD

I was watching *The Big Idea* with Donny Deutsch the other night.
I don't watch much TV but I enjoy his show. Great guests. Interesting insights. And a ton of inspiration. He had on the creator
of *CSI*, a man who used to drive a tram in Las Vegas for $8.50
an hour. His big idea? To write a script for a television show that
married the traditional police show with forensics. That winning
concept has made him rich. It also got me thinking. About screen-
plays and Hollywood writers. They get to write their own stories.
List the cast of characters. And determine how the whole thing
concludes. So do you. True, we can't predict how life will unfold.
In so many ways, the only thing we can expect is the unexpected.
But by writing our stories and then doing our best to act them
out daily, we can get a lot closer to our own Hollywood endings
than those who don't. So many of our professional and personal
desires really can come true—if we write the script. And that's a
beautiful thing.

Many of our professional and personal desires really can come true— if we write the script.

96

ON THE BURDEN OF GREATNESS

I just watched the powerful Hilary Swank movie *Freedom Writers* once again with my kids. The story reminded me of what's most important. At the end of our lives, the only thing that endures is who we became, the difference we made and the love we gave. In one scene, her onscreen father, proud of her inspired work with inner-city kids that other teachers had given up on, told her, "You've been blessed with a burden." I believe the same is true for each of us. As Google co-founder Larry Page once said, leadership really is about "a healthy disregard for the impossible."

We all have talents, resources and capacities that make us special. And with those gifts come responsibilities. To use them. To refine them. To polish them and make them brighter so that we create more value, and so that we elevate the world around us (I adore the Harley-Davidson ad that encourages us to "Leave behind shoes no man can fill"). To forget the burden on you to be great is to neglect the call on your life. And no failure could be bigger than that.

At the end of our lives, the only thing that endures is who we became, the difference we made and the love we gave.

97

LIVE AN INTENSE LIFE

I like my music loud, my coffee strong and my dreams large. I like days with color, people with passion and conversations that call out the best within me. I want to live like there's no tomorrow, achieve the best within me, and love the people in my life like I really mean it. I want to do my part to elevate our world. I want to live with intensity.

What a beautiful word: *intensity*. Live a high-volume life. Play full-out. Take risks. Reach high. Don't look back. Be authentic. Be great. "Live to the point of tears," said novelist Albert Camus. I *so* love that line.

Sure we need to enjoy the journey, tread lightly and balance our courage with striking kindness. But do it all with rare passion, with bravery and with a sparkle in your eye. Do it all with intensity. All of the great ones do.

*Do it all with rare passion,
with bravery and with a sparkle in your
eye. Do it all with intensity.*

98

MAKE YOUR MARK

In an issue of *Best Life* I came across a line from George Clooney: "You only have a short period of time in your life to make your mark." Obvious? Maybe. Yet so true.

It's easy to get so caught up in the daily administrivia that you forget about building your legacy. Easy to become so focused on your problems that you neglect to chase your ideals. Easy to get so pulled into the ordinary pursuits of life that you lose sight of the Extraordinary. Yet, life spins by at an alarmingly fast rate. And if you don't use each day to do even one thing to make your mark and to advance your vision and to become your brilliance, you may miss what truly counts. Makes me think of the words of consultant Richard Leider, who observed, "People over 65 were asked 'if you could live your life over, what would you do differently?' They said three things: I'd take time to stop and ask the big questions. I'd be more courageous and take more risks in work and love. I'd try to live with purpose—to make a difference." That says it all.

If you don't use each day to do even one thing to make your mark and to advance your vision and to become your brilliance, you may miss what truly counts.

99

CREATE YOUR BODY OF WORK

It is early morning as I write this. Relaxing in my library. Listening to Luciano Ligabue, an extraordinary Italian rock star who I got turned on to in Rome and whose music has been shaking the foundation of our home for the past few weeks. And I'm reflecting—about leadership and life.

Just read a little piece in an issue of *Vanity Fair* on Art Buchwald, the writer, who is now 80 and battling kidney failure. Coming close to death brings a human nearer to what's most important in life. Brings tremendous clarity. Strips away all the accessories that we think are so essential when we are younger. Connects us with the Truth (and the truth sets us free, doesn't it?).

He was asked, "What is your idea of perfect happiness?" "Being healthy" was the reply. He was asked, "Which talent would you most like to have?" "Living" was the reply. Then he was asked, "What is your most treasured possession?" "All of my writing—my 32 books and all of my columns." The point of wisdom that you and I can take away? Greatness comes when you create something with your life that is not only bigger than you but outlasts you. Legitimacy and recognition and prestige and material things are all fine and are all very human pursuits. But there's something far more important: Legacy. Making a difference. Having an impact. Creating something special. And meaningful.

What Body of Work will you create over your life so that the generations who follow will know that you've been here? What bold acts and brave moves will you make This Very Moment to let the greatness that slumbers within you come out and visit the light of This Very Day? What will your "most treasured possession" look like? And, at the end, what will you have done with all that talent with which you've been blessed? Just wondering.

Greatness comes when you create something with your life that is not only bigger than you but outlasts you.

100

BIG LIKE MANDELA

I'm reading a beautiful book on Nelson Mandela, a man I admire enormously. A visionary. A freedom fighter. An amazing example of the heights to which human beings can rise. (He invited three of his jailers to his inauguration as president of South Africa—how's that for forgiveness?)

I wanted to share part of the introduction from Bill Clinton, as it speaks to the path you and I—as dreamers, Leaders Without Title and human beings devoted to our best—are on:

"Every time Nelson Mandela walks into a room we all feel a little bigger, we all want to stand up, we all want to cheer, because we'd like to be him on our best day."

Nelson Mandela is an amazing
example of the heights to which
human beings can rise.

101

WILL YOU BE GREAT TODAY?

Someone reading this book today will walk out into their world and do something that will get them to their Next Level of Greatness. Someone near you will make the decision over the coming hours to raise their standards and step up to their highest potential. Someone around you will start something—even if it appears to be a little gesture—that over time will cause breathtaking improvements and results in the way their life looks, in all its dimensions. Why not make that person you?

Forget what anyone's ever told you. Stop listening to the small thinkers. Muffle the voices of the critics. Get to the truth: You are meant to play big with your life. To go out there and be remarkable. No, *extraordinary*. And every time you refuse to listen to that call, you betray yourself.

So honor you. Make this day—and your life—a special and unforgettable one. One tiny step truly can result in gigantic consequences over time. Remember who you truly are, and all you have been built to be: a Leader Without Title, a Rare-Air human being—and someone who made things better. I'll leave you with the words of philosopher Marcus Aurelius, who said, "To live each day as though one's last, never flustered, never apathetic, never attitudinizing—here is the perfection of character." Wonderfully said. I wish you Greatness.

Get to the truth:
You are meant to play big
with your life.

ABOUT ROBIN SHARMA

Robin Sharma is one of the world's leading experts on leadership and personal success. His books, including *The Monk Who Sold His Ferrari* and *The Greatness Guide*, have topped bestseller lists across the globe and have been published in over 40 countries—helping millions of people create extraordinary lives. His work has been embraced by celebrity CEOs, rock stars, top entrepreneurs and royalty. As well as being a much sought after speaker, Robin is also a widely respected success coach for top businesspeople ready to be truly remarkable in all they do.

Robin is the CEO of Sharma Leadership International Inc., a premier training and coaching firm that helps people and organizations get to world class. Clients include Nike, BP, General Electric, NASA, FedEx, IBM and Microsoft. In a recent independent survey of the world's top leadership gurus by leadershipgurus.net, Robin appeared in the top 10—right after Jack Welch. He has been profiled by CNN, the Biography Channel and PBS.

robinsharma.com is one of the most popular resources on the Internet for leadership and success ideas, and offers Robin's blog, robinsharmaTV, along with his acclaimed eNewsletter, The Robin Sharma Report.

To book Robin to speak at your next conference or to discover how Sharma Leadership International Inc. can help you and your organization get to great, visit **robinsharma.com** today.

RESOURCES FOR PERSONAL GREATNESS

Sharma Leadership International Inc. offers a complete range of learning tools and coaching services to help you realize your highest potential and live an extraordinary life. Getting you to world class in your career as well as in your personal life is our mission.

robinsharma.com
ELEVATE YOUR LIFE, TRANSFORM YOUR WORLD™

At this content-rich website you will find Robin's blog, podcasts to keep you inspired and on your best game, robinsharmaTV, The Robin Sharma Report (free monthly eNewsletter), daily inspirational quotes, audio learning programs available for instant download, on demand eCourses, DVDs and inspirational T-shirts, as well as Robin's other books. **robinsharma.com** is also home to a worldwide discussion forum, where you can exchange ideas with other people dedicated to greatness, and to a full listing of upcoming events with Robin.

TheAWAKENING BEST SELF WEEKEND™

Once a year, people from all around the world attend one of the most remarkable and powerful personal development workshops they will ever participate in. The Awakening Best Self Weekend™ (ABS) is a transformational experience that will help you triumph over your fears, reconnect with your highest potential, get clarity on what you want your life to stand for and discover a life-changing system that will help you be your very best. ABS works (and is also one of the most fun learning experiences you'll ever have). For more details, video testimonials and to register for the next ABS Weekend, come and visit **robinsharma.com** today.

Free Audio Download for Readers of THE GREATNESS GUIDE, BOOK 2

To help you get to your greatness quickly, you can now listen to Extraordinary Leadership for free—one of Robin's most popular audio programs (retail value $24.95 USD). In this thought-provoking, potent and practical presentation, you will learn unique ideas to get you to world class, both in your career and within your life. Simply visit **robinsharma.com**, sign up for our free newsletter and download your copy. We only ask one thing of you: that you share this program with others so that, together, we can positively impact many lives.

RESOURCES FOR
ORGANIZATIONAL GREATNESS

"Though Sharma rejects the guru label, it's hard not to think of this CEO that way." —*Publishers Weekly*

Sharma Leadership International Inc. offers a wide range of products and services to help you increase the leadership performance of your people. For information on Robin Sharma's keynote presentations and workshops as well as to learn more about his results-oriented e-learning programs, visit robinsharma.com.

Grow The Leader™ is a revolutionary and strikingly powerful web-based training program that helps employees lead without title and organizations get to world class. Many of the world's best-known companies are using Grow The Leader™ to develop leadership cultures, realize the highest performance potential of their staff, unleash innovation and create an extraordinary team that wins in their market.

Based on The 8 Best Practices of World-Class Leaders, **Grow The Leader**™ will help your people:

- *think, feel and behave like world-class leaders.*
- *focus their actions on activities that create spectacular results.*
- *show personal responsibility, renewed passion and lasting engagement.*
- *become superb team players that collaborate and help the organization succeed.*
- *seize the opportunities change presents.*
- *awaken natural creativity and talent for innovation to drive constant improvement.*
- *discover what the best performers in business do to achieve work-life balance and show personal leadership.*

For more information on how **Grow The Leader**™ and our other resources can get your organization to world class, visit **robinsharma.com**.

Give the gift of
GREATNESS

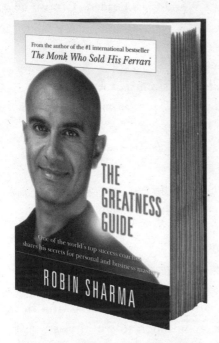